BEBOPSCALES
FORJAZZGUITAR

Master Soloing with Major, Minor and Dominant Bebop Scales for Jazz Guitar

ELEONORASTRINO

FUNDAMENTALCHANGES

Bebop Scales for Jazz Guitar

Master Soloing with Major, Minor and Dominant Bebop Scales for Jazz Guitar

ISBN: 978-1-78933-388-6

Published by www.fundamental-changes.com

www.fundamental-changes.com

Over 12,000 fans on Facebook: **FundamentalChangesInGuitar**

Instagram: **FundamentalChanges**

For over 350 Free Guitar Lessons with Videos Check Out

www.fundamental-changes.com

Cover Image Copyright: Author photo, Giovanni Esposito, used by permission.

Contents

Introduction

Welcome to my first book for Fundamental Changes, which explores how to learn and use bebop scales for jazz guitar.

The idea of tension and release is an integral part of the sound of jazz. Tension is created when the notes of a melodic line briefly move *outside* of the harmony of a tune, and release comes when the note choices bring us back *inside* the harmony. This is the sound of bebop – characterised by intricate melodic lines that weave around the chord changes – and mastering this sound is the challenge before every aspiring jazz guitarist.

Often, bebop scales have been taught in an overly complicated way, but in this book, we're keeping things simple. A bebop scale is just a regular scale with *one approach note added*. This one extra note makes bebop scales incredibly useful for creating the sense of tension and release we want. They are what help us to compose melodic lines that include chromatic runs – one of the distinctive features of bebop. Where this note is placed depends on the type of scale, and there are bebop scales for major, minor and dominant harmonic situations.

That is bebop in a nutshell, but it's very important to learn the scales in the correct way, and understand how to apply them creatively. My aim here is to give you a solid method for learning each scale, and to show you how to use them to create the jazz vocabulary you've heard used by the masters of the artform.

I hope you enjoy it!

Eleonora

Get the Audio

The audio files for this book are available to download for free from **www.fundamental-changes.com.** The link is in the top right-hand corner. Click on the "Guitar" link then simply select this book title from the drop-down menu and follow the instructions to get the audio.

We recommend that you download the files directly to your computer, not to your tablet, and extract them there before adding them to your media library. You can then put them onto your tablet, iPod or burn them to CD. On the download page there are instructions and we also provide technical support via the contact form.

For over 350 free guitar lessons with videos check out:

www.fundamental-changes.com

Over 12,000 fans on Facebook: **FundamentalChangesInGuitar**

Tag us for a share on Instagram: **FundamentalChanges**

Chapter One – The Major Bebop Scale

We're going to start by learning the bebop scale based on the Major scale. All the examples in this chapter are illustrated in the key of C Major, so it will be easy to spot the "bebop note" in the notation. When we begin to play licks using this scale, spotting the bebop note will help to grow your understanding of how to apply this scale in a musical context.

First, let's look at the effect of adding an approach note to the C Major scale.

The notes of C Major are:

C – D – E – F – G – A – B

The C Major Bebop scale adds a passing note between the 5th (G) and 6th (A) scale intervals to produce this arrangement of notes:

C – D – E – F – G – Ab – A – B

We now have an eight-note scale that contains a b6 (Ab) tension note.

Let's hear how this alters the sound of the scale. Exercise 1 shows the C Major Bebop scale in position three, with the root note on the fifth string. Play up and down the scale a few times to get used to the sound of the added approach note.

Exercise 1

So that you can begin to experiment with this scale straight away, here's an easy reference diagram for the C Major Bebop scale in third position. The bebop note is indicated with a hollow circle. Explore this shape for a few minutes and see what kind of musical ideas it suggests to you. In a moment, we'll learn the scale in a more structured way, but for now, just get used to the sound of it.

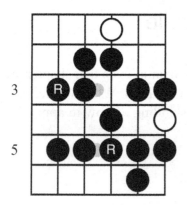

In jazz, it's very common to solo using passages of constant 1/8th notes and this is the where the bebop scale becomes so useful. Since it's an eight-note scale, you'll immediately notice that it sounds very smooth when played over a set of chord changes and it's much easier to construct 1/8th phrases to fill a bar.

The bebop scale also helps us to develop the skill of playing chord tones on the strong beats of the bar (the down beats) and chromatic or "passing notes" on the weaker beats (the off beats). We'll discuss this more in due course.

Now we turn our attention to learning the scale, which we will do in two ways:

1. As CAGED scale shapes

2. As arpeggios built from the chord tones of its parent chord, Cmaj7

If you want to use the bebop scale effectively for soloing, it's important to know it inside out. Understanding it scalically from the root note, and as a set of four arpeggios built from chord tones, will give you the right foundation. First, let's look at the scale shapes.

Scale shapes

Now that we've heard the basic sound of the major bebop scale, we're going to learn it in five box positions across the neck. These positions reflect the CAGED system of organisation, which is a great way of applying any scale across the range of the neck, based around five simple chord shapes.

Because we are working in the key of C Major, we'll begin with the lowest CAGED shape first, then work our way up the fretboard. For each scale, I'll illustrate the corresponding chord shape with a diagram.

The lowest available position (without using open strings) is the "A shape". Below is an "A" shape Cmaj7 chord diagram, and Example 1a shows the C Major Bebop scale ascending and descending in this zone of the neck.

Cmaj7 "A" Shape

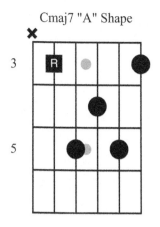

Example 1a

Notice that I also included the available notes on the sixth string before completing the scale where it began.

Moving up the fretboard, the next zone contains the "G" shape of Cmaj7. As a chord, this can be tricky to play and still include the low root note on the sixth string. It's completely optional to play it, but it's important to know where the root note is located, indicated by a hollow square.

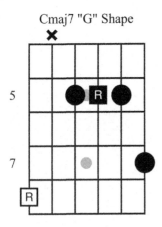

Cmaj7 "G" Shape

Here's the C Major Bebop scale in this zone, played in 5th position.

Example 1b

Next, in 8th position is the "E" shape of Cmaj7.

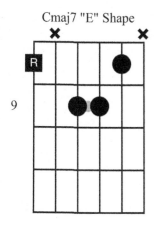

Cmaj7 "E" Shape

And here is the corresponding bebop scale shape.

Example 1c

Next, we have the "D" shape chord and scale, played in 9th position. You may have noticed that whenever we need to move slightly out of position to play the scale smoothly, we do so with a slide up or down, so that there is economy of movement.

Cmaj7 "D" Shape

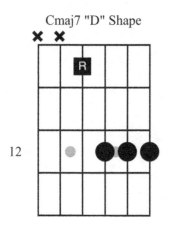

Example 1d

Lastly, here is the "C" shape with its corresponding scale pattern, played in 12th position.

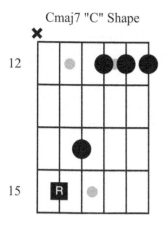

Cmaj7 "C" Shape

Example 1e

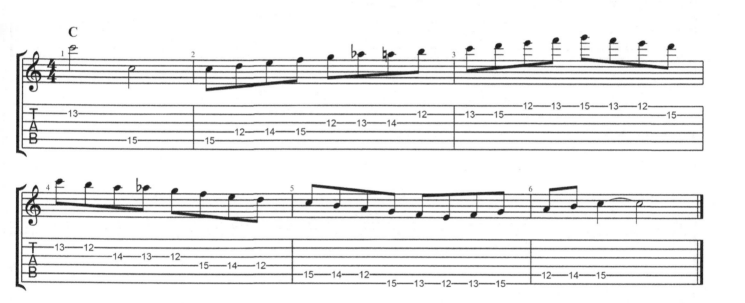

Before we move on to explore the scale through arpeggios, let's take a look at a few easy licks. These are very simple ideas using the C Major Bebop scale, but they are useful for embedding the sound of the bebop approach note in our ears. At the end of the chapter, there are some much more challenging licks, so you'll have plenty to work on during your practice times.

Each of these lines can be played over a static Cmaj7 chord, but will also work well in a major ii V I context, as indicated below. Try them out.

Example 1f

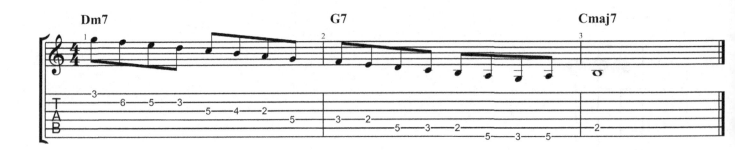

Example 1g

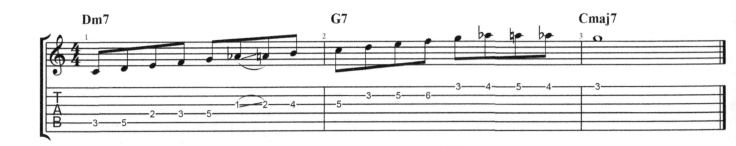

Example 1h

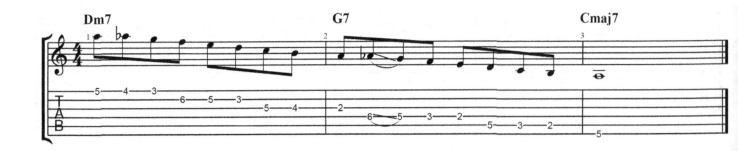

Example 1i

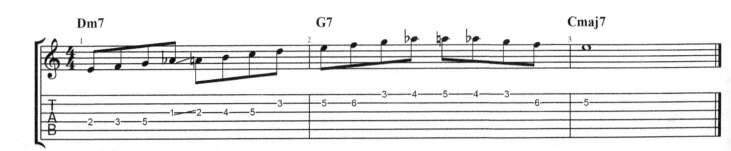

Arpeggios

Next we're going to practice the major bebop scale by combining it with arpeggios built from the parent chord of Cmaj7. We need to know the scale shapes across the fretboard, because this will help us to construct runs that move between positions, but understanding how the scale relates to arpeggios will add more musicality and depth to our vocabulary.

First, let's remind ourselves of the four arpeggios contained within the Cmaj7 parent chord.

Cmaj7 is constructed C (root), E (3rd), G (5th), B (7th).

We can build a four-note arpeggio from each chord tone using the notes of the C Major scale, as shown in Example 1j.

In bar one, the notes spell a Cmaj7 arpeggio (C E G B)

In bar two, they spell an Em7 arpeggio (E G B D)

In bar three, they spell a G7 arpeggio (G B D F)

And in bar four they spell a Bm7b5 arpeggio (B D F A)

(NB: notice the extra note in bar three. When playing the G7 arpeggio, it's normal practice to "resolve" the F note to the E chord tone of Cmaj7, to avoid a clash when playing over this chord).

Example 1j

Now we're going to play some exercises that bring together these arpeggios with the major bebop scale. Although I call them "exercises" they are melodic exercises. Each one is a useful melodic idea in its own right.

In this first exercise we ascend each arpeggio shape shown in the previous example, then descend the bebop scale. Here's how that sounds:

Example 1k

We can modify the previous exercise by "displacing" the first note of each arpeggio up an octave, then jumping back to play the rest of the line as before.

Example 1l

Let's try the exercise one more time, but this time we'll descend each arpeggio, then double back to descend the bebop scale.

Example 1m

These movements are helping you to begin building a library of bebop phrases.

You'll notice that the previous three exercises were all played using the "A" shape of the bebop scale, based around 3rd position (illustrated back in Example 1a).

I won't spell out all the exercises here, but in your practice sessions, make it your goal to work out the arpeggio/bebop scale phrase combinations for *all* the other CAGED scale shapes. If you work at this, over time you'll master the scale right across the fretboard and do so in instantly useable phrases.

Try focusing on just one CAGED shape per practice session, rather than trying to tackle the whole fretboard at once. That way, you are more likely to commit the ideas to muscle memory.

Once you have worked through that process, you can try this!

The following exercise uses the "E" shape of the bebop scale (see Example 1c for a reminder) and mixes up the approach to playing the arpeggio/bebop scale combinations. Here we have descending, ascending and octave displaced arpeggios all together.

Example 1n

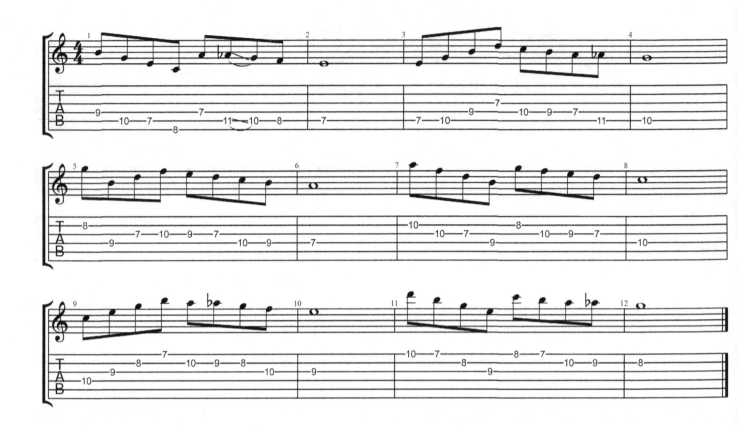

If you work carefully through all of the previous exercises, and are diligent in practicing this idea in every CAGED position, you'll be able to mix and match these phrases all over the neck. I will show you one more example of how to do this, then it's over to you. Here is this idea played using the "D" shape of the scale (see Example 1d).

Example 1o

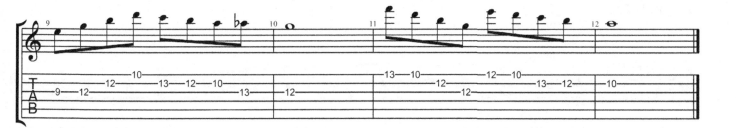

Moving on, let's look at how these arpeggio/scale combinations can be fused together to form longer melodic phrases. First, play through the following lick:

Example 1p

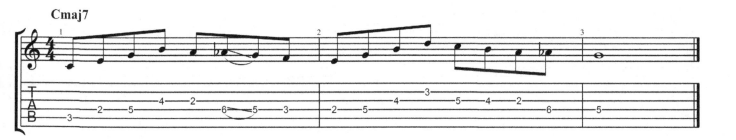

Played over a static Cmaj7 chord, this line combines the arpeggio phrases that first appeared in bars 1-2 of Example 1k. The result is a perfectly formed, two-bar bebop line that weaves around the Cmaj7 harmony.

But the same exact line works perfectly well if we play it over the ii V I sequence in C Major. Here's how it sounds:

Example 1q

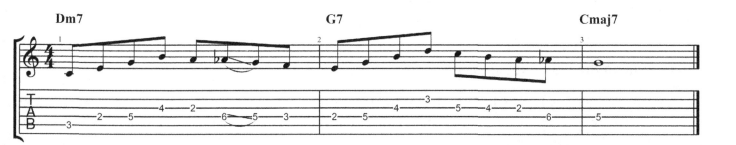

Let's work through this idea of fusing together arpeggio/scale combinations to form longer bebop lines, and use other zones of the fretboard to do so. Remember, we can ascend or descend the arpeggios, and also displace the first note by an octave. Play through the following three examples and notice the approaches being used in each one.

Example 1r

Example 1s

Example 1t

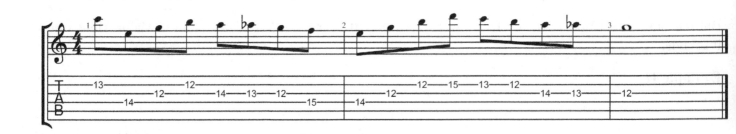

Harmonising the major bebop scale

So far, all the ideas we've looked at, and the melodic phrases we've created, have come from traditional harmony. We've used the major scale as the *source* of our melodic information, and added just one extra note to form the bebop major scale.

But what if we take this new, eight-note bebop scale and treat *it* as the source?

We know that harmonising the major scale results in a set of diatonic arpeggios, but what happens if we harmonise the bebop scale with its additional note?

In fact, this is exactly what countless jazz greats have done throughout the history of the music, and the results of doing so are both surprising and musically rewarding. Let's take a closer look at this idea and work through its musical application.

First, let's remind ourselves of the notes of the C Major Bebop scale:

C – D – E – F – G – Ab – A – B

Now let's harmonise that scale into chords, in the same way we would the major scale, by stacking the intervals in 3rds (every other note).

The first chord is formed using the notes C E G A, which spells C6.

The second chord is formed using the notes D F Ab B, which spells Ddim7.

In fact, when we harmonise the entire scale, what is produced is a series of alternating C6 and Ddim7 inversions. Here is the full harmonised scale:

C	D	E	F	G	Ab	A	B
C E G A	D F Ab B	E G A C	F Ab B D	G A C E	Ab B D F	A C E G	B D F Ab
C6	Ddim7	C6	Ddim7	C6	Ddim7	C6	Ddim7

The result of this process is an important sound in modern jazz. When you listen to some of the amazing melodic lines played by musicians like Charlie Parker or Sonny Stitt, they are drawing from this idea. It is also a feature of the playing of the great Wes Montgomery, and informs the thinking behind many of his licks and chordal ideas, where he effortlessly blends diminished ideas with straight arpeggios.

Because this idea can be used for comping (Wes style) as well as for creating more interesting melodic lines, it's important to have a good understanding of the chord shapes that arise from the harmonised bebop scale. The following exercises show you how to play them across all string sets.

First, on the lower strings.

Example 1u

Next, on the middle string set.

Example 1v

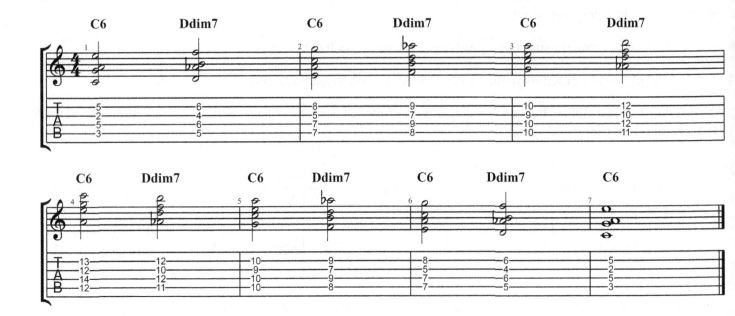

And, finally, on the top strings.

Example 1w

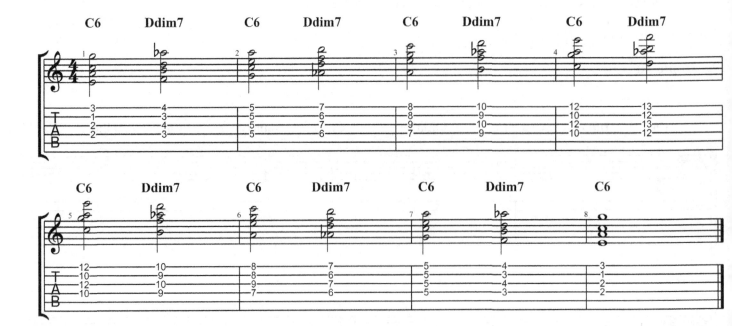

Now we have an understanding of the sound that is created by harmonising the bebop scale, we can work with it in a similar way to before, spelling out each chord sound as an arpeggio.

The following exercise begins in 3rd position, with the C root note on the fifth string, then spells out the four-note arpeggio for each degree of the C Major Bebop scale.

Play through this several times and familiarise your ears with this new sound.

Example 1x

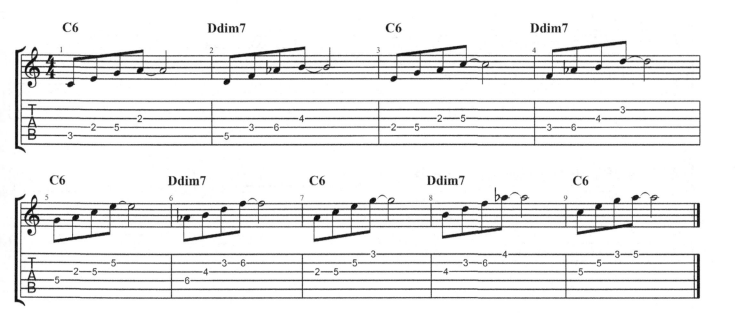

As we've done before, we can take each of these arpeggios and combine them with a descending bebop scale run. You may notice that in a couple of places, a chromatic (non-scale) tone has been added for convenience, to make a descending line a little smoother.

Example 1y

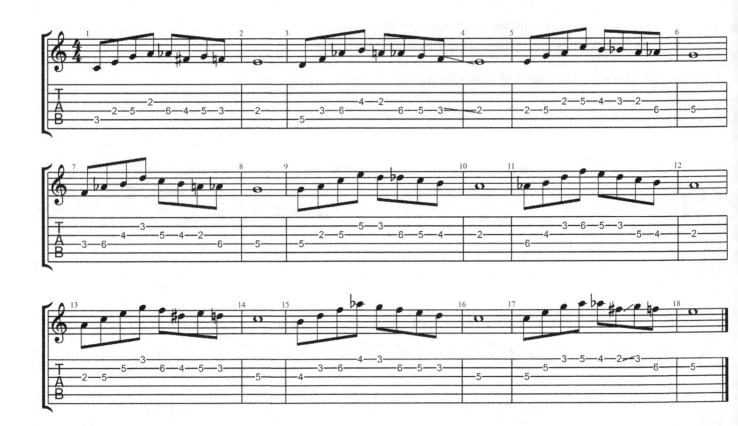

Although I won't spell out every possible exercise for you here, you can see the immense potential of this idea, if you took the time to work through each way of playing an arpeggio (ascending, descending, and displaced octave) in each of the five CAGED scale shapes, it would provide an incredible wealth of melodic ideas and vastly increase your knowledge of the fretboard. Of course, this represents a massive amount of learning, but it is a process you can chip away at during your practice sessions.

Developing bebop vocabulary

Now we are going to look at how all these ideas translate into bebop vocabulary. We'll begin with some relatively easy licks played over the major ii V I chord sequence, then move on to some much more challenging ideas that you can work on longer term.

First, here are ten swung 1/8th note licks played at a medium tempo. The ii V I backing track I used to play over is included as part of the audio download for this book. You can use it to practice these licks and also to explore your own ideas.

Think of these examples as vocabulary building exercises. We've discussed the rules of the language and learned how to express certain key phrases, but there is no better way to become fluent at a language than by speaking it.

This first example begins with a four-note phrase using the harmonised major bebop scale. The notes spell out a C6 arpeggio. The second group of four notes in bar one use an *enclosure*. The idea is that scale or arpeggio tones are "enclosed" by scale tones and/or chromatic approach notes. The F# note that appears here is targeting the G chord tone on the fourth string, 5th fret. That G note is the 3rd of Cmaj7, but when played over a Dm7 chord creates a Dm11 sound.

Example 1z

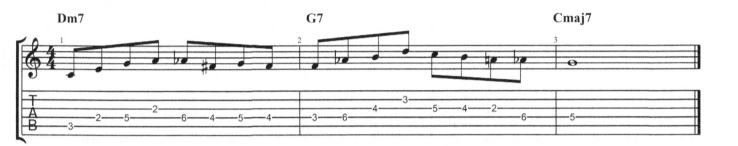

Like the previous lick, this idea is played using the "A" CAGED form. The lick opens with a C6 arpeggio again, but this time played as an inversion (G A C E). When playing an idea like this, take a moment to visualise the CAGED shape it is based around. Practice "seeing" the chord shape, then the scale notes that sit around it.

When improvising, we can target any chord or scale tone, approaching it chromatically from above or below, as long as we hit a chord/scale tone on a strong beat of the bar. For example, the last two notes of bar two are targeting the E note on beat 1 of bar three – the 3rd of Cmaj7.

Example 1z1

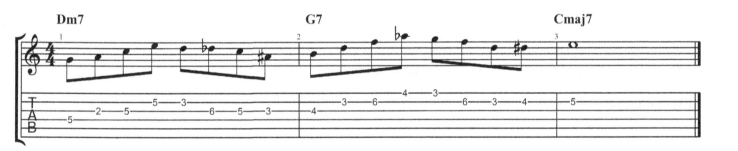

Bar one of this lick includes another enclosure idea. We are targeting an E note on beat 4, which is the 3rd of Cmaj7, or implies a Dm9 sound over the D minor chord. The E is enclosed by a scale tone above (F) and a chromatic note below (D#).

Of course, the Ab bebop note is used in this lick, but you should be beginning to hear how it is possible to weave around the harmony by introducing *other passing notes* where appropriate, Charlie Parker style.

Example 1z2

The next lick uses only the arpeggios created by harmonising the C Major Bebop scale. Bar one begins with a C6 arpeggio, which is repeated using an inversion. Then, in bar two, we play the Ddim7 arpeggio from its root note, then repeat it up an octave. The lick resolves to a C Major scale tone, rather than a chord tone in this instance. The A note on the first string implies the underlying harmony is Cmaj13.

Example 1z3

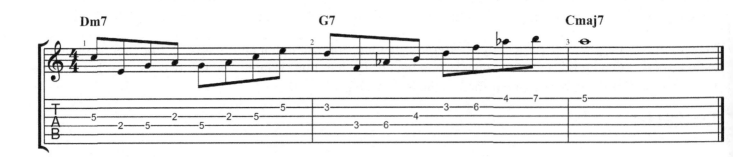

This lick begins with an inverted C6 arpeggio, and is followed by a chromatic run down. The Ab bebop note falls on beat 4& of bar one and is targeting the root note of G7 on beat 1 of the next bar.

Example 1z4

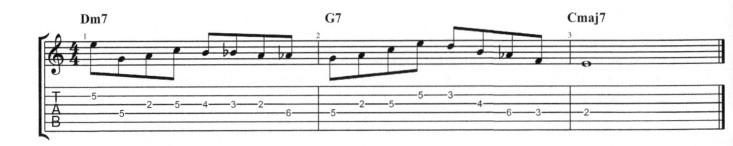

The next example is a simpler idea that uses the unembellished C Major scale for the whole lick, apart from the bebop note at the end of bar two, which targets the 5th of Cmaj7.

Example 1z5

Here is a similar idea featuring a chromatic descent to target a chord tone. It ends on the 7th of Cmaj7.

Example 1z6

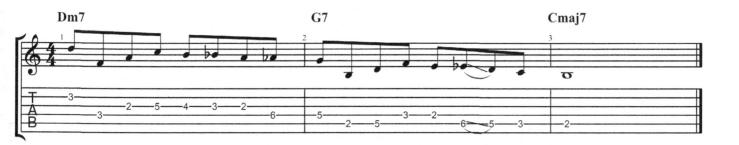

The next example is a staple idea of bebop language that you will almost certainly have heard played before! Bar one is all C Major scale notes, apart from the last note, which is a chromatic approach to the B note on beat 1 of bar two.

In bar two, the first four notes spell a G7 inverted arpeggio, launched from the 3rd (B). The last note of the inverted arpeggio leads neatly into the Ab bebop note on the first string, 4th fret. Next, an additional passing note (Bb) is introduced to create some added tension. When played over the G7 chord, the Ab and Bb notes create b9 and #9 intervals respectively.

Example 1z7

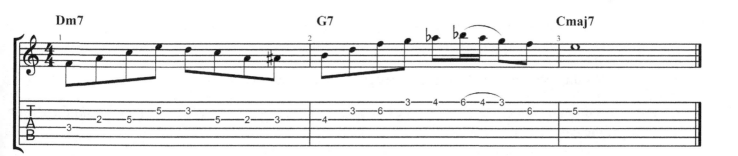

The next lick repeats the Gb9/G#9 idea in the lower register in bar two.

Example 1z8

The first four notes of this idea use the C Major scale to spell an Fmaj7 arpeggio. When played over a D minor chord, the Fmaj7 arpeggio creates a Dm9 sound. This is followed by a straight Dm7 arpeggio.

In bar two, a chromatic run down targets the G chord tone that falls on beat 3.

Example 1z9

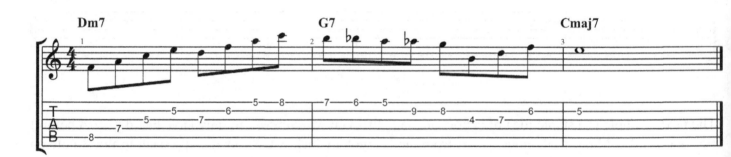

These simple licks have given you the flavour of how *all* bebop licks are created. Remember the following principles:

*   Visualise a CAGED chord form on the neck

*   Visualise the arpeggio/scale notes that sit around it (refer back to the exercises and diagrams earlier in the chapter)

*   Combine and mix up simple arpeggio and scale ideas (ascend an arpeggio, descend the bebop scale; descend an arpeggio and jump back to descend the scale, etc)

*   Invent melodic ideas that move between arpeggio- and scale-based ideas

*   Begin to add in *additional* chromatic notes in order to target chord or scale tones that fall on the strong beats of the bar

There is one more important idea to take on board at this point.

The bebop scale is not just intended for use over the parent chord. I.e. we don't have to save the C Major Bebop scale exclusively for playing over Cmaj7 chords. We can use it for the whole major ii V I sequence, and the notes of the scale will imply subtly different harmonies over each chord.

With all these principles in mind, to close out this chapter we're going to change up a couple of gears to play some much more challenging licks at a faster tempo. These are mostly 1/16th note ideas and use all the melodic ideas we've discussed so far.

They are played over the same major ii V I backing track, so these lines are *much* quicker than before! However, don't be put off by that. Learn them very slowly and treat them as musical etudes. Commit the movements to muscle memory before you attempt them at a faster tempo.

The main goal here is to get the sound of the bebop language in your ears. The more you work with these ideas, the more you will begin to hear similar lines in your head, and that is our ultimate goal: to get you *thinking* like a bebop player.

This first advanced line appears very complex on the face of it, but let's break it down. In bar one there are several chromatic approach notes used, besides the Ab bebop note. However, the whole line is based around the "G" CAGED shape. Here is a quick reminder of it:

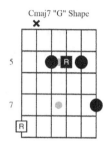

Cmaj7 "G" Shape

Notice that the first four notes in bar one all target the B note of this shape that sits on the first string, 7th fret. The next four notes target a G scale tone; the next four target the Ab bebop note; and the final four target a B scale tone.

When played over a Dm7 chord, in order, these tones create colourful 11th, #11 and 13th intervals. In addition, I've already "broken" one of our guiding principles, because I allow passing notes to fall on strong beats in this lick. However, rules are made to be bent (or occasionally broken!) and it is fine to do this sometimes, as long as you have a clear destination in mind and you eventually resolve your phrase to a chord tone on a strong beat.

In bar two, a similar idea is at work in this more intervallic sounding phrase. Every fourth note is a G7 chord tone that is being targeted, apart from the last note of the bar which targets the G scale tone that falls on beat 1 of bar three.

Example 1z10

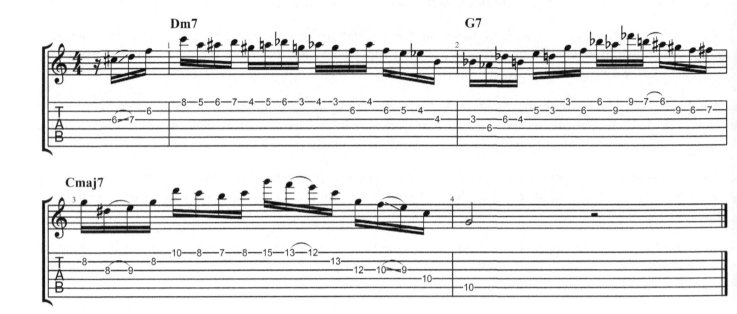

Bar one of this lick shows how to develop a bebop lick that moves between CAGED shapes. The line begins in the "G" form, like the previous lick, then ascends into the "E" form for the latter half of the bar. You can see that the two shapes connect easily to one another, joining together two zones of the fretboard.

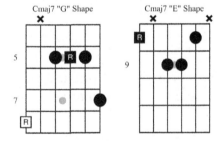

This lick also uses a common modern jazz device that is used to add tension to a lick.

In bar one, the first four notes are all C Major scale tones. The subsequent four notes come from executing a *sidestepping* movement. In other words, playing a scale shape either a half step above or below its true position.

Here, we are using the "G" shape scale pattern then shifting it *up* a half step, before moving into the "E" shape to play scale tones once more. This idea is commonly known as an "outside-inside" line. We began inside, sidestepped to create tension, then moved back inside – all as part of a continuous 1/16th note line.

Example 1z11

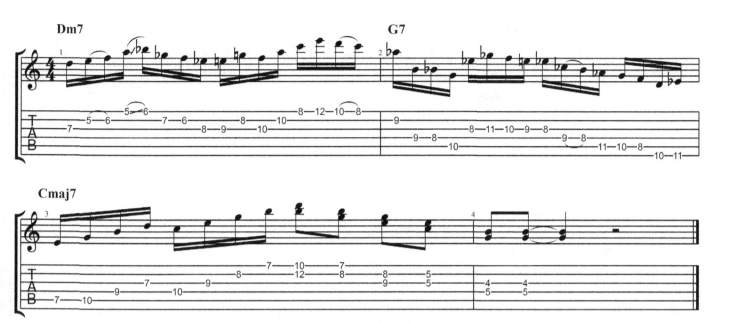

In bar one of the next example, the line ascends the CAGED "E" form in 8th position, then jumps up into the "C" form to descend for the second half of the bar. The Ab bebop note does not make an appearance in this bar – instead we are playing passing notes purely based around this CAGED shape.

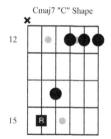

Bar two does contain the bebop note, and this time the idea is to cascade downwards, based around the "C" shape, with a repeating rhythmic phrase. The end of bar two uses an approach note from a half step below to target the G note (3rd of Cmaj7) that falls on beat 1 of bar three.

Example 1z12

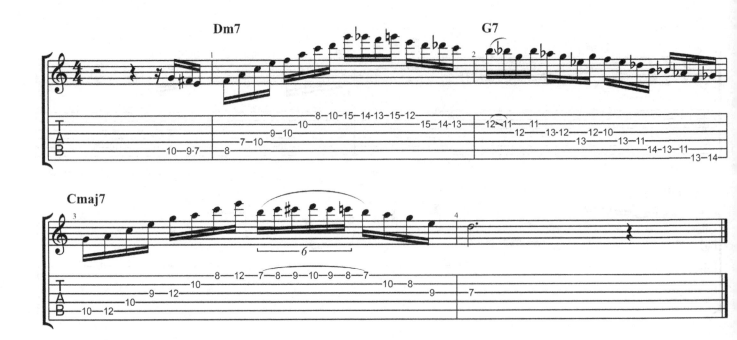

Example 1z13 is a motif-driven lick that begins with a scalic line that contains a series of chromatic approach notes. Then, in bars 2-3, we play a repeating motif idea.

The phrase at the beginning of bar two states the musical motif. All the notes are C Major scale tones. The exact same lick is then shifted up a minor 3rd (a distance of three frets, not including the starting note). Repeating a lick, note for note, in a different zone of the fretboard can produce some surprising results. Here, it produces an Eb chromatic note, the Ab bebop scale note, and the rest of the notes are scale tones.

In bar three, the motif is shifted upward again, this time by a major 3rd (four frets), where it falls into the "C" form of CAGED. The last note of this phrase is altered because it's the start of a chromatic run down.

Example 1z13

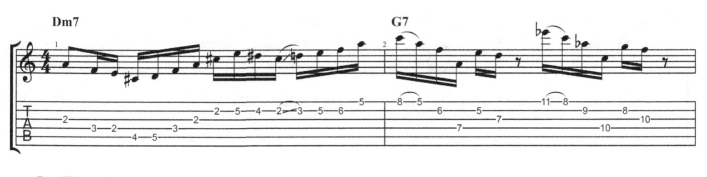

Next, we have a line where the phrasing continually rises and falls. Bar one uses the "G" form and mostly scale notes until the second half, when passing notes are introduced. The target is the C scale tone at the beginning of bar two.

The four-note phrase at the beginning of bar two is a very common way to highlight the bebop note. This part of the line uses several passing notes to ascend until we hit the target B note (the 7th of Cmaj7) at the beginning of bar three. It's worth reminding ourselves here, it's amazing how much tension we can introduce into a line as long as we hit a chord tone on a down beat. An audience will forgive the most outside sounding line, as long as we anchor the harmony with chord tones on the strong beats.

Pay special attention to the descending phrase over the Cmaj7 chord, as it uses the Ab bebop note four times, each time on the up beat. The notes that fall on the down beats spell an inversion of Cmaj7 (B E C G, including the first note of bar four).

Example 1z14

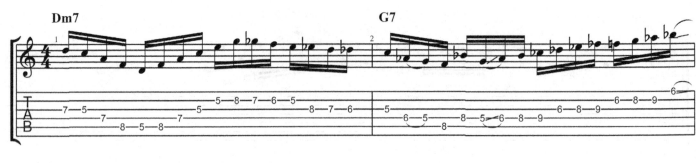

Example 1z15 begins with a line that weaves around C Major scale tones using passing notes. Again, the bebop note is not present, and the idea comes from working around the CAGED shapes. The first three notes come from the "G" form, before we jump quickly into the "A" form for the rest of the phrase.

In bar two, the four-note opening phrase begins with the Ab bebop note, then ascends a straightforward G major triad. Over G7, the effect is to create a G7b9 sound, and the b9 is a tense note to begin the phrase on.

The next four-note phrase begins with Bb and Ab notes – an idea we've used before, which immediately creates the #9 and b9 tension. The remaining two notes are a chord tone, B (the 3rd of G7) and Eb. The Eb represents the b13 or #5 of G7. There's no need to puzzle over where these note choices come from – they all sit within the "A" shape below. Remember, any of the notes surrounding the shape are possibilities for creating melodic ideas. We just need to exercise some taste and play ideas that appeal to us.

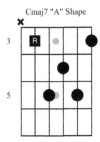

Cmaj7 "A" Shape

Example 1z15

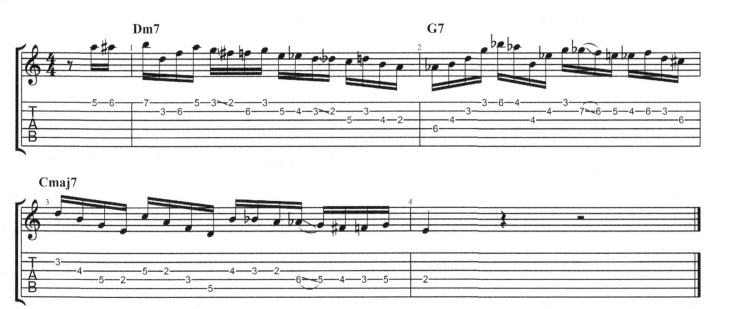

After the opening phrase of bar one, this line uses a chromatic descent that moves from a high E down to a C note that falls on beat 3. As we've seen, it's common in bebop to have *multiple* chromatic approach notes that lead to a target destination and this is a prime example of how that can work in practice.

In bar two, you can probably see that this is a shape-based lick, with the same pattern being repeated on the G and B strings as the line moves between the "G" and "E" forms. The point of the idea is to create a lot of tension, then land on the B chord tone on the first string on beat 3.

Example 1z16

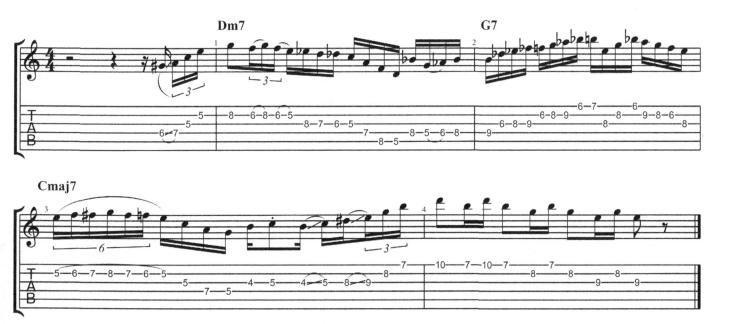

This line begins with two inverted Fmaj7 arpeggios played over the Dm7 chord then, after a lead-in E note, a long chromatic descent begins that concludes when we hit the B chord tone of G7 on beat 1 of bar two.

In bar three, the Ab bebop note is used as a fast passing note in the 1/16th note triplet phrases.

Example 1z17

Here is another motif-based idea for you to try. The motif is a nine-note phrase that mixes 1/8th and 1/16th notes to create a swinging rhythm that floats over the groove. The first time the motif is stated over Dm7, all the notes belong to the C Major scale. When the motif is repeated over the G7 chord, just one note is changed and the Ab bebop note is added, which as you know by now creates a G7b9 sound.

Either statement of the motif would have worked perfectly well played over the Cmaj7 chord in bar three, but to add some sonic surprise we add a *sidestep* movement and lower it by a half step.

The effect of this movement is to begin the line with an F# note – a very tense sounding #11 interval over Cmaj7. In fact, the F# appears five times throughout the line. Even though all the other notes are scale tones, this tense note radically changes the character of the line, giving it a more contemporary jazz sound.

The entire lick is based around the "C" CAGED form.

Example 1z18

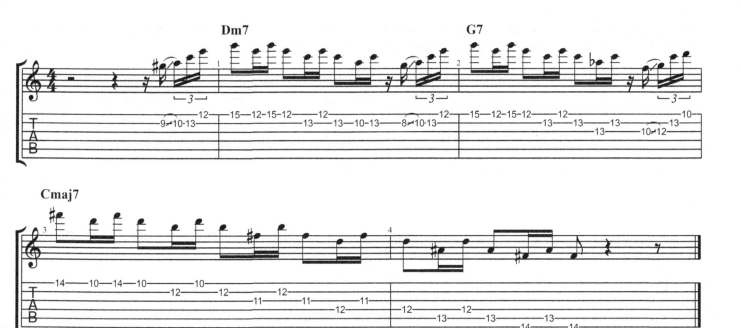

To conclude this chapter, here is a line based around the "C" form. The opening phrase comprises nearly all scale tones, apart from a passing Eb. In bar two, chromatic approach notes are introduced to give the line more tension. Once again, the note choices come from their proximity to the "C" shape.

Example 1z19

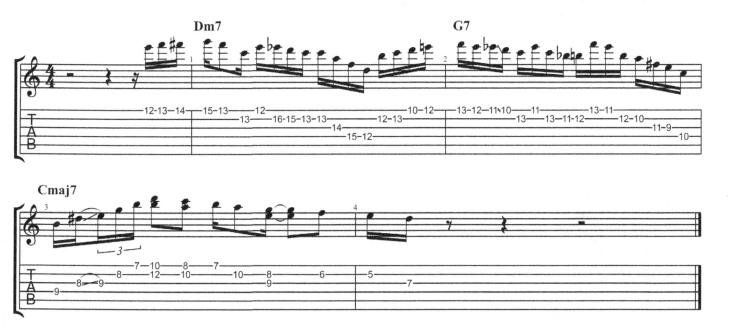

In the next chapter, we're going to look at the minor bebop scale and learn lots more bebop language.

Chapter Two – The Minor Bebop Scale

In this chapter we're going to learn the minor form of the bebop scale. All the examples in this chapter use C minor for illustration. First, let's visualise the scale with the added bebop note.

There are a few variations of the minor bebop scale, all created in the same manner, by adding a passing note between two degrees of a minor scale. Here we are using the C Melodic Minor scale as our source (other options include bebop scales based on the harmonic minor and Dorian scales). Students of the great Barry Harris will have heard him refer to the melodic minor bebop as the "minor sixth diminished scale".

The notes of C Melodic Minor are:

C – D – Eb – F – G – A – B

In the minor bebop scale, the bebop note is placed between the 5th and 6th intervals of the scale, introducing a b6 interval:

C – D – Eb – F – G – Ab – A – B

We now have an eight-note scale that contains a b6 (Ab) tension note.

Now, let's hear the scale with the added tension note.

CAGED scale shapes

As you might guess, we're going to learn this scale using CAGED minor shapes, so that we can play it across the range of the fretboard, which will prepare us to improvise with it in any zone of the neck.

Example 2a shows the C Minor Bebop scale played from its root on the fifth string. This pattern corresponds to the "A" form of CAGED and, in C minor, is the lowest position in which we can play the scale without using open strings.

Play the scale ascending and descending several times to get familiar with the sound of the added approach note.

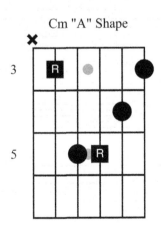

Cm "A" Shape

Example 2a

Example 2b shows the C Minor Bebop played from its root note on the sixth string, using the CAGED "G" form.

Cm "G" Shape

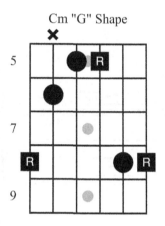

Example 2b

In Example 2c we use the "E" form of CAGED to play C Minor Bebop with its root note also on the sixth string.

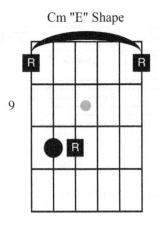

Cm "E" Shape

Example 2c

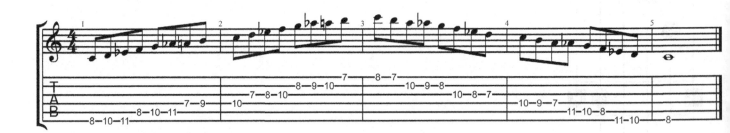

Now we move on to play the first of the two shapes that occupy the higher register. Here is C Minor Bebop played from the root on the fourth string, using the "D" form of CAGED.

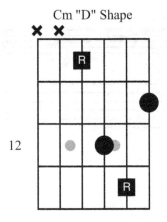

Cm "D" Shape

Example 2d

And finally, the scale using the "C" CAGED form, with its root note on the fifth string.

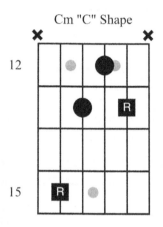

Cm "C" Shape

Example 2e

Your goal should be to know these shapes inside out, so that when improvising you're able to move freely between them and create melodic ideas right across the neck. Why not use these five shapes as a warm-up at the beginning of a practice session, or before a gig? That way you can achieve the dual goals of warming up the fingers and drilling these shapes into muscle memory.

As in the previous chapter, before we move on, let's play a few simple licks that use this scale with its added b6 note. This will help to embed the sound of it in our ears before we move on to drill it using arpeggios.

Each of these lines can be played over a static Cm7 chord, but will also work over a "quick" minor ii V i sequence, as indicated in the notation (i.e. the ii V movement takes place in one bar, as it often does in jazz standards, like the tune *Yesterdays*). Check them out below.

Example 2f

Example 2g

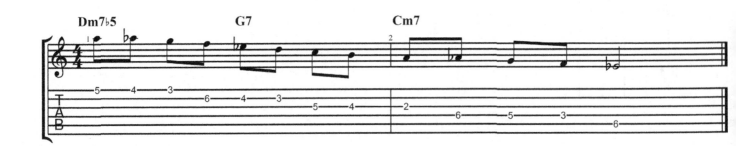

Example 2h

Example 2i

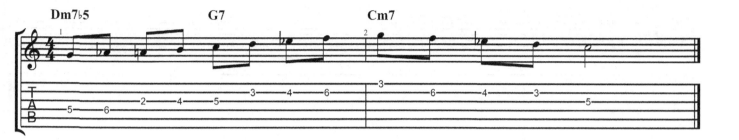

Example 2j

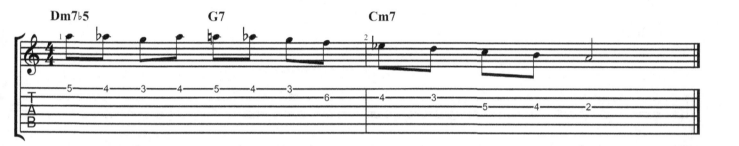

Arpeggios

Next we're going to practice the minor bebop scale in the context of arpeggios built from the parent chord. We are using the C Melodic Minor scale as the "source" for our bebop minor scale, so in this instance the parent chord will be CmMaj7.

CmMaj7 is constructed C (root), Eb (b3), G (5th), B (major 7th).

We can build a four-note arpeggio from each chord tone using the notes of the C Melodic Minor scale, as shown in Example 2k.

In bar one, the notes spell a CmMaj7 arpeggio (C Eb G B)

In bar two, they spell an EbMaj7#5 arpeggio (Eb G B D)

In bar three, they spell a G7 arpeggio (G B D F)

And in bar four they spell a Bm7b5 arpeggio (B D F A)

Example 2k

Now we're going to play some exercises based on these arpeggios similar to Chapter One. Each of these exercises is designed to reinforce the connection between the arpeggio and the bebop scale.

To begin, we ascend each arpeggio, then descend with the minor bebop scale.

Example 2l

In the next exercise, each arpeggio is played descending then we jump back to the same place as in Example 2l and descend the bebop scale as before. You can hear that these exercises form useful phrases that could be used as licks in their own right, so learn them thoroughly.

Example 2m

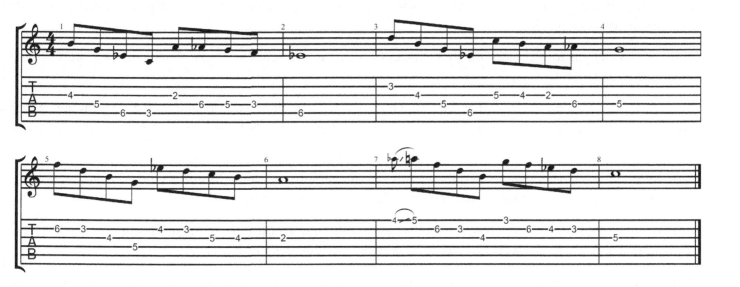

Let's return to the idea of Example 2l. We will ascend the arpeggio and descend the bebop scale as before, but this time we'll create an intervallic jump by displacing the first note of the arpeggio up an octave. Here's how it sounds.

Example 2n

These movements are helping you to build your library of bebop phrases. Each one forms a solid, reliable lick, because it is a combination of strong arpeggio notes and scale tones that has a clear beginning and end. Playing them will automatically improve your phrasing.

You'll notice that the previous arpeggio exercises were all played using the "A" shape of the CAGED system (based around a 3rd position C minor chord with its root note on the fifth string) which we saw back in Example 2a. During your practice sessions, work with the other four CAGED positions and repeat the arpeggio drills in those zones of the neck.

Now we can begin to elaborate on these ideas to play more interesting licks. I will mix up the CAGED positions to play them.

Each of these licks follows a similar format. There is a lead-in phrase that begins in the pick-up bar, which anticipates the first chord of the minor ii V i. Then, each phrase ends in bar three on a chord tone of the C minor chord.

NB: Although we have already noted that chord I in the key of C Melodic Minor is CmMaj7, in practice this is most often played as a straight Cm7 in jazz standards, as indicated here.

This first example begins with an enclosure. We play a chromatic note (Bb) to begin the phrase, then play a G scale tone, the Ab bebop note, then land on an A scale note on beat 1 of bar one.

Bar one begins with a descending inverted Bm7b5 arpeggio that moves into a descending scale movement. Bar two leads with a CmMaj7 arpeggio and mimics the phrasing of bar one with a descending run that ends on the Eb chord tone.

Example 2o

We are using this idea of targeting beat 1 in all of these short examples. Here, the target is an Eb scale tone.

In Chapter One, I mentioned an important principle regarding bebop scales and now is a good time for a reminder. We don't have to reserve the bebop scale to use only over the parent chord i.e. C Minor Bebop for Cm7 or CmMaj7 chords. We can use it for the whole minor ii V i sequence. When played over the ii and V chords, the scale tones will just create different harmonic effects.

We can achieve the same effect by mixing and matching the arpeggios produced by harmonising the scale. In bar one, for example, the first four notes spell an Ebmaj7#5 arpeggio (the arpeggio built from the b3 of CmMaj7). When this arpeggio is layered over the Dm7b5 (D F Ab C) chord, it suggests the more complex harmony of Dm7b5b9.

Example 2p

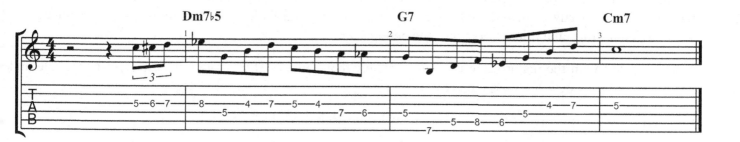

In bar one of this line, we play a straight CmMaj7 arpeggio over Dm7b5. Again, the notes (C Eb G B) have interesting consequences for the harmony. The B, for instance, implies a Dm13b5. Superimposing one arpeggio over another is an easy way to instantly create a new sonic texture.

Example 2q

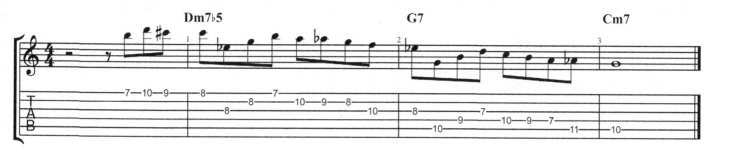

This example anticipates the V chord by playing a G7 arpeggio over Dm7b5. Over the G7, a Bm7b5 arpeggio is superimposed, which creates a G9 sound.

Example 2r

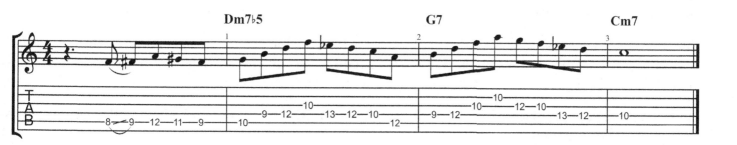

Harmonising the Bebop Minor Scale

Until now, the ideas we've looked at, and the melodic phrases we've played, have all come from traditional harmony. We've used the melodic minor scale as the *source* of our melodic information, and we've added one passing note to form the minor version of the bebop scale.

Just as we did with the major scale in Chapter One, what happens if we take our new eight-note scale and harmonise it into a new set of arpeggios?

First, let's remind ourselves of the notes of the C Minor Bebop scale:

C – D – Eb – F – G – Ab – A – B

Now let's harmonise that scale into four-note chords, in the same way we would the regular C Melodic Minor scale to create 7th chords, stacking the intervals in 3rds.

The first chord is formed using the notes C Eb G A, which spells C minor 6.

The second chord is formed using the notes D F Ab B, which spells Ddim7.

If we were to examine the C Major and C Melodic Minor scales side by side, we would see that they only have one note different. C Melodic Minor has an Eb as its third degree, compared to the E of C Major.

So, similarly to the major scale, when we harmonise C Minor Bebop, the result is a set of alternating inversions. The diminished 7 inversions this process creates are exactly the same as those derived from C Major Bebop, but the Eb note results in a set of Cm6 inversions.

The table below shows the whole harmonised scale.

C	D	Eb	F	G	Ab	A	B
C Eb G A	D F Ab B	Eb G A C	F Ab B D	G A C Eb	Ab B D F	A C Eb G	B D F Ab
Cm6	Ddim7	Cm6	Ddim7	Cm6	Ddim7	Cm6	Ddim7

Again, this melodic information forms an important part of the sound of modern jazz harmony. Listen to players like John Coltrane and you'll hear him cycling through series of four-note cellular patterns in his solos.

We're going to take this idea and work with it using *just* the C minor 6 chord. In practice, this is the most useful sound from the harmonised scale. The minor 6 is incredibly versatile for soloing over modal tunes in the jazz repertoire, much like Coltrane did, and also for use in minor ii V i sequences.

First of all, we're going to learn inversions of Cm6 across all string sets, then we'll briefly drill these inversions with a couple of exercises.

First, here are the inversions of Cm6 played on the lower four strings, ascending and descending.

Example 2s

Now play through this set of inversions on the middle four strings.

Example 2t

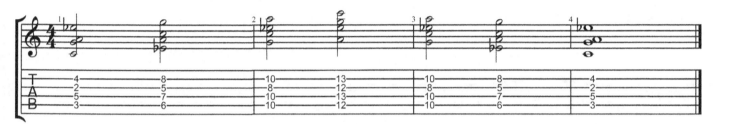

And finally, on the top four strings.

Example 2u

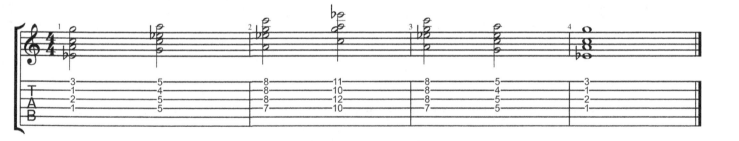

The next exercise plays all four inversions of Cm6 in arpeggio form, based around third position.

Again, we're using just the "A" form of CAGED with its root note on the fifth string, but you should work through the other CAGED positions and make sure you know how to play the arpeggio in all zones of the neck.

Example 2v

Now let's try a slightly different arpeggio exercise to the ones we played earlier in the chapter. Here, we will ascend each inversion of the arpeggio and descend with the bebop minor scale. However, in order to make a complete phrase, then land on a chord tone of Cm6 on the first beat of the next bar, we need to add one additional chromatic passing note into each phrase. Listen to the idea first, then play through it.

Example 2w

Finally, before we move on to playing some more advanced licks with the minor bebop scale, try this exercise.

Starting on each chord tone of the Cm6 arpeggio, ascend the minor bebop scale and end on the note you began with i.e. C to C, Eb to Eb, etc.

Note that when we ascend the scale from G in bar five, we run out of notes, so an F# approach note completes the pattern and gets us to G.

Example 2x

Developing bebop vocabulary

So far, we have learned the minor bebop scale across the neck using CAGED forms, and examined it in both arpeggio and scale form. Now it's time to translate those ideas into usable bebop language.

As in the previous chapter, we'll begin by playing some easy 1/8th note licks that demonstrate the minor bebop sound, played over a minor ii V i. After that, there will be a series of more demanding 1/16th note licks.

First, ten swung 1/8th note ideas. There is a minor ii V i backing track with the audio download for the book. You can use this to practice these ideas and jam out your own using the minor bebop scale.

After a chromatic walk up the second string, this line begins by targeting a G scale tone on beat 1 (which happens to be the 11th of Dm7b5). The four-note phrase ends on an Ab note, which is the bebop note, but also the b5 of the chord. In bar two, the phrasing of bar one is echoed, and a similar idea is played over the first part of the bar, where the 11th of G7 is highlighted.

Example 2y

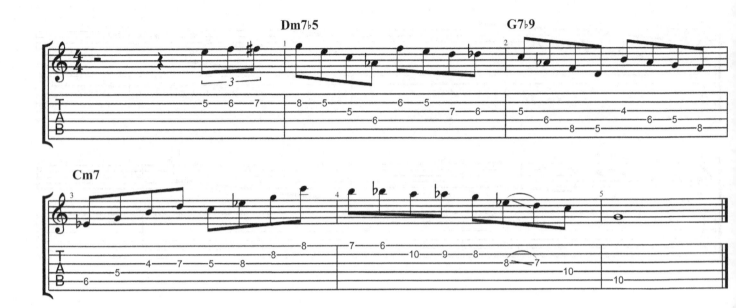

This idea begins with a long chromatic run down in bar one. The target note is the D on beat 1 of bar two, the 5th of G7. The phrasing idea in bar two should be very familiar to you by now. The first four notes are a Dm7b5 arpeggio, played by displacing the root note up octave. The ii and V chords are so closely linked that we can play G7 arpeggio ideas over Dm7b5, and Dm7b5 arpeggio ideas over G7. They both work well.

Example 2z

Next, a line that begins with a scalic descent that includes some passing notes. In bar two, you'll play one of the most popular substitution ideas in modern jazz.

When we see a dominant chord, we can play a minor scale or minor arpeggio a half step above its root note. In other words, here we can play Ab minor ideas over the G7 chord. This is a quick hack used by many jazz musicians to easily access the notes of the Altered scale. Here we are using an Abm9 arpeggio, and the notes create the same sonic effect as if we were playing the G Altered scale.

Example 2z1

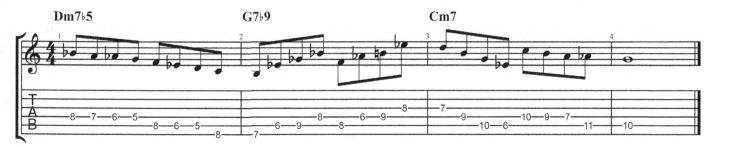

In the next lick, making a slight modification to a Dm7b5 arpeggio (lowering its F note to Eb) gives the lick some brief suspended tension and, overall, implies the sound of Dm11b5. It's a sound I like, and you'll see that it crops up in other places in my playing.

Example 2z2

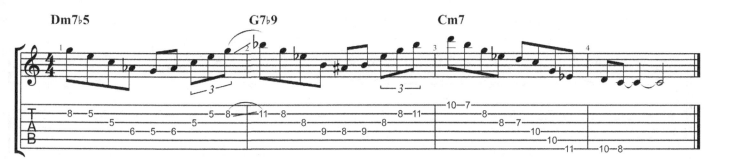

The next line contains another example of sidestepping in bar three. Visualise the Cm7 barre chord that sits in eighth position. The first four notes come from playing around that shape but shifting it up a half step to C#m7. The lick resolves back down to the regular Cm7 shape. To hear and understand this idea better, hold down both the C#m7 and Cm7 barre chords. You'll see that the notes of the lick are all accessible to play around these shapes with your fourth finger.

Example 2z3

Here's an idea that is all about ascending on the first string, in order to give the line momentum and cover a wide range of the fretboard. Let me draw your attention to another modern jazz idea that occurs at the beginning of bar one.

When it comes to playing over the minor 7b5 chord in a ii V i, rather than viewing it as the ii chord, and playing notes from the parent key (in this case, C Minor), jazz musicians will often view it as the vi chord from another key instead.

Dm7b5 is the vi chord in the key of F Minor.

This means that, for a brief moment, we view Dm7b5 as chord vi in the key of F Minor, not chord ii in the key of C Minor. And, for that bar, we can switch to F Melodic Minor (F G Ab Bb C D E) to create our melodic ideas, then switch back to C Minor Bebop for the subsequent bars.

This is a core idea of bebop harmony and, to remember it, you can think: whenever I see a m7b5 in a minor ii V i, I can play the melodic minor scale a minor third above (i.e. the movement from D to F. Dm7b5 = F Melodic Minor). Experiment with this sound in your next practice session over the minor ii V i backing track.

Example 2z4

Here's another example of how to use this idea over the minor 7b5 chord. This lick begins with a descending F Melodic Minor scale run over the Dm7b5 chord.

Example 2z5

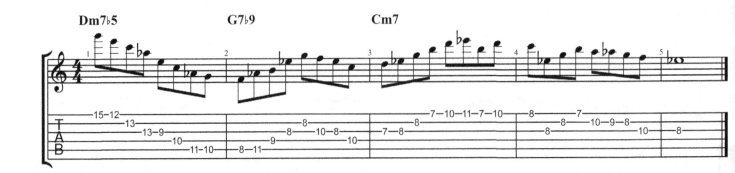

This line begins with a run down the C Minor Bebop scale. The opening four-note phrase is repeated in the lower octave, but the final note is altered, so that it becomes a chromatic approach note and the G root note of G7 falls on beat 1 of bar two, rather than at the end of bar one.

Example 2z6

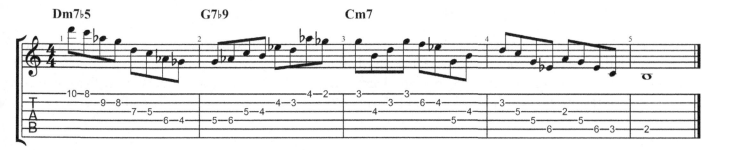

To create more interest in our lines, string skipping provides a way to play wider intervals. This is a motif-type line that uses that same phrasing throughout. The phrase over the G7b9 chord begins with a sidestepping idea (visualise a C#m7 barre chord) before resolving to notes around the Cm7 barre in position eight.

Example 2z7

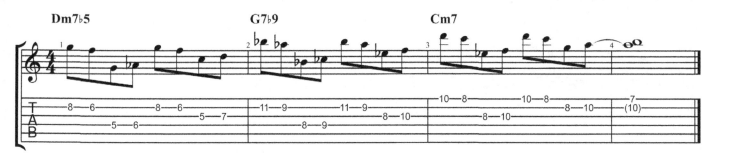

Lastly, here's one more example of using F Melodic Minor (bar one) to create interest over the Dm7b5 chord. After a chromatic lead-in note, then a chord tone of G7, the F Melodic Minor idea continues over the V chord in bar two. In bar three, we switch to C Melodic Minor for the remainder of the lick.

Example 2z8

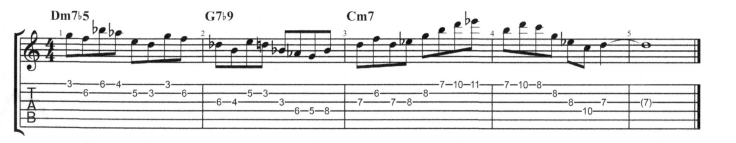

Now let's move onto some more challenging lines.

This set of five licks predominantly use 1/16th notes. Don't worry if, at present, the tempo is too fast for you. Treat each idea as a mini etude. You are learning the shape and sound of the scale and beginning to understand how it works over the chord changes. You can play these lines super slow until you absorb them into muscle memory and gradually speed up. The important thing is that you are learning bebop vocabulary. Also, feel free to just steal part of a line, if you hear a phrase that appeals to you, and add it to your internal lick library straight away.

In bar one of the first 1/16th note example, the line begins with C Minor Bebop scale notes, but then introduces some F Melodic Minor tensions. The whole line based around the "A" form of C minor, so a good way to learn and understand it is to play the "A" shape Cm7 barre chord at the 3rd fret and visualise how these notes sit around it. The rest of this line is based around C Minor Bebop with a few passing note additions.

Example 2z9

This example begins with a line based around the "G" shape of C minor. The overall intention here is to create a downward cascading effect. In bar one, we start with a chromatic run down that targets the A scale tone at the 5th fret. It's a tension note over Dm7b5, but the Ab that follows resolves it. The next phrase comes from F Melodic Minor, then the line moves back into C Minor Bebop with some passing notes to fill out the line.

Bar two, over the G7 chord, continues with the bebop scale. In the top register, we're using the "D" CAGED shape to build the line around.

In bar three, the descending line has a similar cascading feel. Pay attention to the notes that fall on the downbeats and you'll see that they are all strong Cm6 chord tones.

Example 2z10

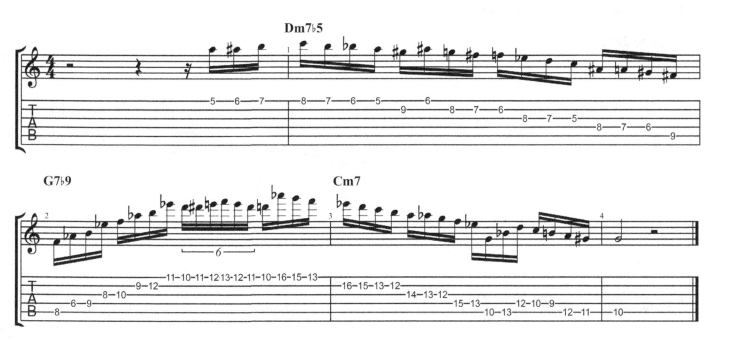

Example 2z11 begins with a descending scale sequencing lick. The idea here is to create a four-note motif and repeat the phrasing, descending a scale tone each time on the first string. The scale of choice here is F Melodic Minor. In bar two, the descending/ascending line is structured so that G7 chord tones fall on the strong beats.

Example 2z11

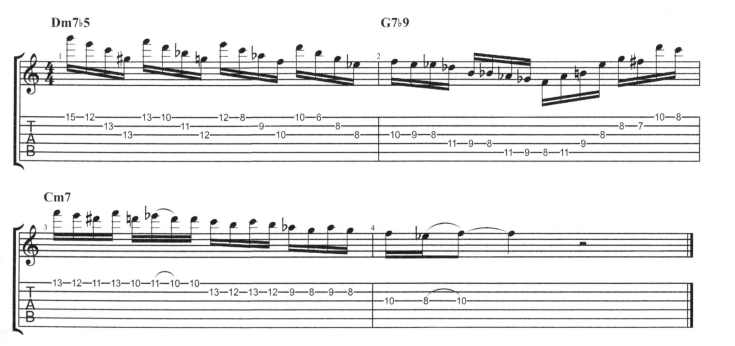

Example 2z12 features another example of playing Ab minor ideas over the G7 chord to access the sound of the G Altered scale. There are some chromatic passing notes here too, but the core idea is based around the Ab Melodic Minor scale (Ab Bb B Db Eb F G).

Example 2z12

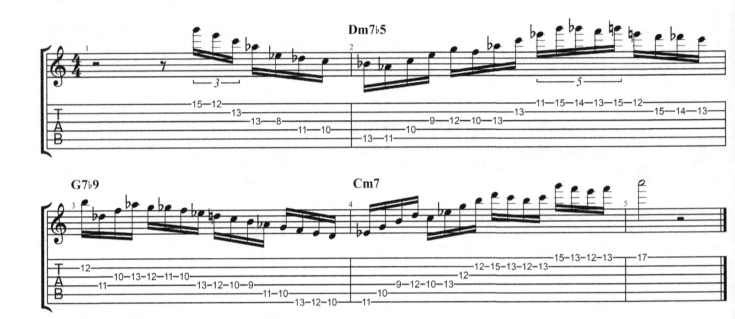

Here is one final minor bebop idea that you should treat like an etude and learn slowly to commit the movements to memory. Again, the opening line uses the F Melodic Minor scale. Over the G7 chord in bar two, the first eight notes come from the Ab Melodic Minor scale, then F Melodic Minor is hinted at again, but this lick is more about repeating the note intervals and their phrasing than it is about sticking to a specific scale. Bar three opens with a classic minor bebop lick you'll have heard Pat Martino and others play.

Example 2z13

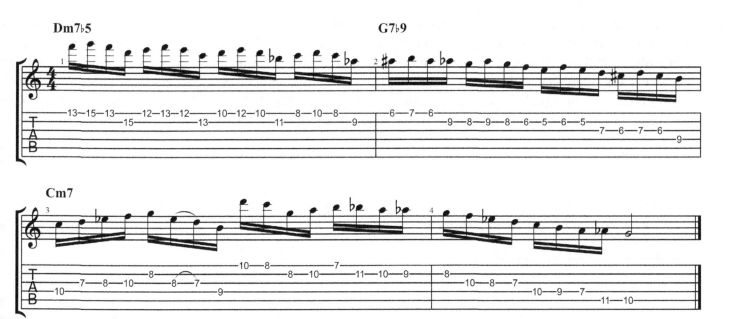

Spend as much time as you can learning the longer licks as etudes and pull out any short ideas that appeal to you and incorporate them into your playing as licks. In the next chapter, we'll look at the popular dominant bebop scale.

Chapter Three – The Dominant Bebop Scale

Now we turn to perhaps the most popular of the three main bebop scales – the dominant bebop. It's the most frequently used because so much of the vocabulary of modern jazz is focused on the dominant chord. Jazz standards are full of ii V I movements, with the dominant chord as the pivotal point in the harmony, and jazz musicians will often change the *quality* of chords from minor to dominant, to create another opportunity to use the dominant bebop sound. Then, there are tunes based on the Rhythm Changes, with its cycle of dominant chords, and dominant based modal tunes, etc!

All the examples in this chapter use the chord C7 for illustration. First, let's visualise the scale with the added bebop note.

C7 is the V chord in the key of F Major, so the scale that fits C7 perfectly is C Mixolydian (like playing an F Major scale beginning and ending on the note C).

The notes of C Mixolydian are:

C – D – E – F – G – A – Bb

In the dominant bebop scale, the bebop note is placed between the 7th and the octave/root intervals of the scale, which introduces a major 7 (B) in addition to the existing b7 (Bb):

C – D – E – F – G – A – Bb – B

This give us an eight-note scale that contains a major 7 (Bb) tension note.

Let's explore the sound of the scale and learn it using the five CAGED positions on the neck.

CAGED scale shapes

First, play the scale ascending and descending to get used to the placement of the additional passing note. Exercise 3a uses the "A" form of CAGED played from the fifth string root.

C7 "A" Shape

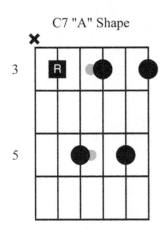

Example 3a

Example 3b shows the C Dominant Bebop scale played from its sixth string root using the "G" form of CAGED.

C7 "G" Shape

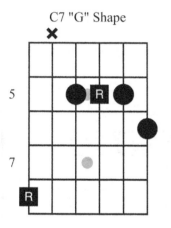

Example 3b

For the next zone of the fretboard we are using the "E" form of CAGED to play C Dominant Bebop from its sixth string root at the 8th fret.

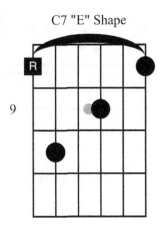

C7 "E" Shape

Example 3c

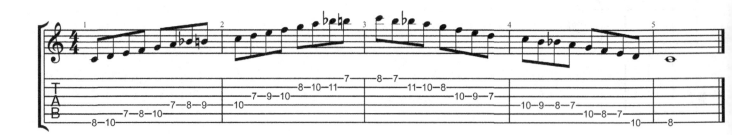

Now we move on to play the two CAGED shapes that occupy the higher register. First, C Dominant Bebop played from its root on the fourth string, using the "D" form.

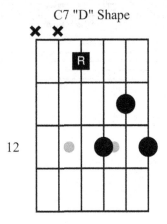

C7 "D" Shape

Example 3d

And the scale using the "C" CAGED form with its root notes on the fifth and second string.

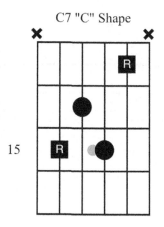

C7 "C" Shape

15

Example 3e

Spend some time practicing C Dominant Bebop in all five zones of the neck. You are probably already familiar with the Mixolydian scale, but the addition of the new passing note creates a new dynamic and changes the fingering options for the scale, which takes a bit of getting used to.

Before we go any further, let's play a few simple licks to help embed the sound of the scale in our ears. These lines can be played over a static C7 chord, or in the context of a ii V I in the key of F Major, where C7 is the V chord. These lines are purposely quite linear in their approach, so that you can clearly hear the effect of the passing note.

Example 3f

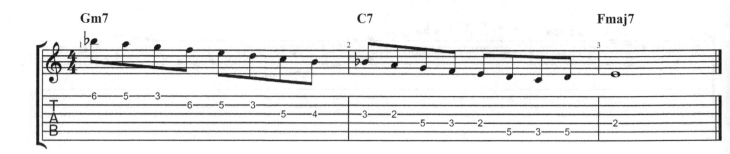

Example 3g

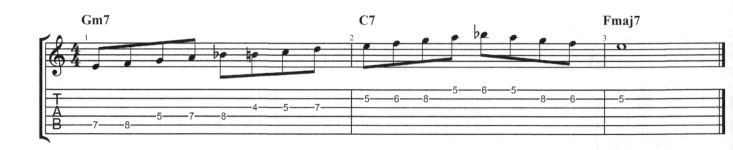

Example 3h

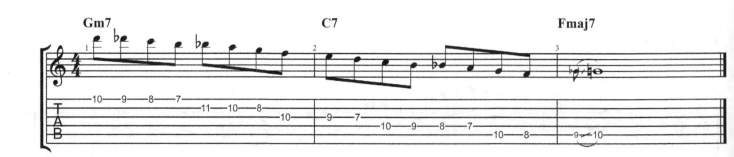

Example 3i

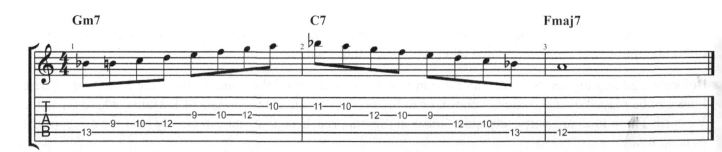

Arpeggios

Let's move on to drill the dominant bebop using arpeggios built from the parent chord. We know that C7 is the V chord in the key of F Major, so the chords that result from building arpeggios from each chord tone of C7 are found in that key signature.

In bar one, the notes spell a C7 arpeggio (C E G Bb)

In bar two, they spell an Em7b5 arpeggio (E G Bb D)

In bar three, they spell a Gm7 arpeggio (G Bb D F)

In bar four, they spell a Bbmaj7 arpeggio (Bb D F A)

Example 3j

Now play through the following arpeggio exercises to reinforce the shape and sound of the scale. You played an exercise similar to this in the previous chapter. We ascend each arpeggio, then descend the bebop dominant scale, but with the addition of a chromatic passing note to create a phrase-like idea.

Example 3k

Next, play each arpeggio ascending again, but displace the first note up an octave.

Example 3l

In the next exercise, each arpeggio is played descending, then we jump back to play the same descending pattern as the previous exercise.

Example 3m

Using Example 3m as your template, work through all five CAGED positions repeating the exercise. In the example below, I demonstrate this using the "G" form, but you should work your way through the others until you can play the exercise fluently in all zones.

Example 3n

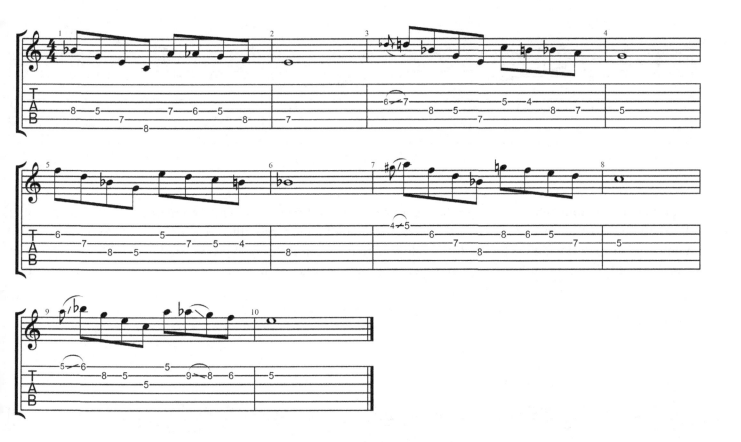

Now that we are getting familiar with the sound and shape of the scale, let's move onto the next stage of the process and play some authentic bebop licks. The lines mix and match CAGED positions on the fretboard. Notice that each line ends on a strong chord tone, which could work over a static C7 chord, or the I chord (Fmaj7) in a major ii V I.

This first line contains some passing notes in addition to the bebop note, but notice that in bar one, three chord tones of Gm7 (G Bb D F) fall on the down beats and the same occurs in bar two over C7 (C E G Bb).

Example 3o

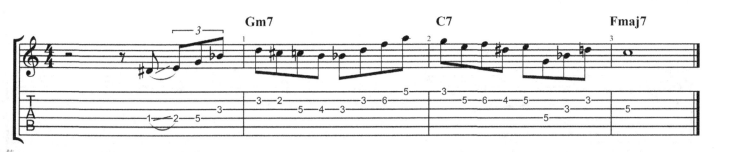

In the next example, the bebop note (B) is played on beat 4& of bar one and resolves to the Bb note at the beginning of bar two (the b7 of C7).

Example 3p

Example 3q is staple bebop language. In the pickup bar, the line begins with an enclosure. The target note is the E on beat 1 of bar one. First, we play a scale tone above the target, then a scale tone below it, and finally a half step chromatic approach note from below. The first four notes of bar one spell an Em7b5 arpeggio (an arpeggio built from the 3rd of C7). This stack of notes can also be interpreted as an inverted Gm6 arpeggio. Bar two begins with an inverted C7 arpeggio.

Example 3q

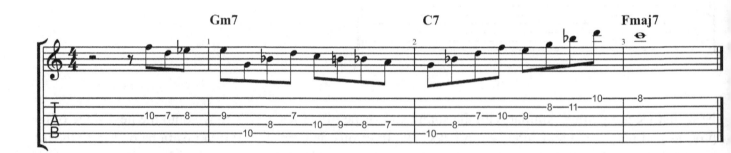

The next idea begins with a chromatic run down to reach the target note of F in bar one, where the first four notes spell a Gm7 arpeggio. The next four notes include the bebop note at the end, which again is used to resolve to a Bb note in bar three.

Example 3r

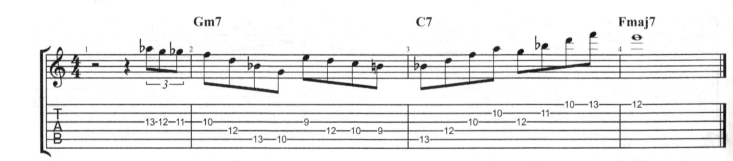

Harmonising the dominant bebop scale

As we've done in previous chapters, let's now turn to look at harmonising the dominant bebop scale.

The C Mixolydian scale has been our source of melodic information, and we added one passing note to that scale to form the C Dominant Bebop scale. Let's see what happens when we harmonise this new eight-note scale into four-note arpeggios.

The notes of C Dominant Bebop are:

C D E F G A Bb B

If we stack the intervals in 3rds, the first chord is formed from the notes C E G Bb, and spells the C7 chord.

The second chord is formed using the notes D F A B, which spells D minor 6.

If we continue and harmonise the whole scale, we end up with a series of alternating C7 and Dm6 inversions:

C	D	E	F	G	A	Bb	B
C E G Bb	D F A B	E G Bb C	F A B D	G Bb C E	A B D F	Bb C E G	B D F A
C7	Dm6	C7	Dm6	C7	Dm6	C7	Dm6

Just as we did with the minor 6 sound in the previous chapter, we are going to focus on working with just the C7 inversions. First of all, we'll learn them across all string sets, beginning with the four lowest strings.

Example 3s

Next, play the inversions ascending and descending on the middle four strings.

Example 3t

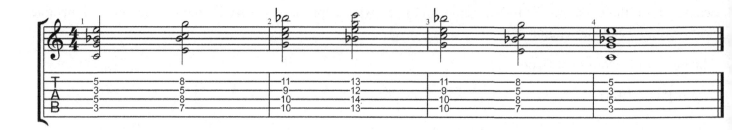

And, finally, on the top four strings.

Example 3u

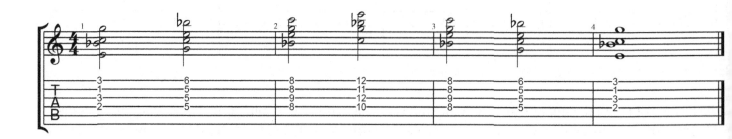

Now we're going to take these C7 inversions and drill them with some exercises.

This first exercise plays all four inversions of C7 in basic arpeggio form, based around third position.

We're using just the "A" form of CAGED with its root note on the fifth string, but you should work through the other CAGED positions and make sure you know how to play the arpeggio in all zones of the neck.

Example 3v

Next we'll repeat an exercise we did with the C minor 6 arpeggio in Chapter Two. We will ascend each inversion of the arpeggio and descend with the dominant bebop scale. But, in order to play a complete phrase and land on a chord tone of C7 on the first beat of the next bar, we'll add an extra chromatic passing note.

Example 3w

Here is one more arpeggio-based exercise for you, before we move on to play some melodic phrases. This time we will ascend the dominant bebop scale from each chord tone of C7. Notice that each phrase begins and ends on the chord tone.

Being able to launch a scale from any interval of a chord is a great skill to develop in your playing. It's all too easy, when playing over changes, to always begin phrases from the root of the chord or scale. However, if we can play scalic passages starting from the 3rd, for example, our lines will still perfectly fit the harmony but sound much less predictable.

Example 3x

Developing bebop vocabulary

Now you've learned the dominant bebop scale across the neck using CAGED shapes, and examined it in both arpeggio and scale form, it's time to translate these ideas into some authentic bebop vocabulary.

We'll begin by playing a series of easy 1/8th note licks that spell out the dominant bebop sound over a major ii V I in the key of F Major.

Practice these to the F Major ii V I backing track in the audio download, and also compose your own ideas using the scale and arpeggio forms we've studied.

In bar one, this phrase begins by climbing the bebop scale launching from an E note to spell an Em7b5 arpeggio. When played over a G minor chord, these four notes imply a Gm6 harmony. The next four notes included the bebop note in a chromatic descent.

In bar two, notice that the opening four notes use the same pattern as the start of bar one, but now we are launching from the fourth string, 5th fret, to play a Gm7 arpeggio. The bebop note is used to resolve to an Fmaj7 chord tone in bar three. The great thing about the placement of the bebop note in the dominant bebop scale is that it is always a half step below the root note of the I chord, which helps a lot when resolving phrases.

Example 3y

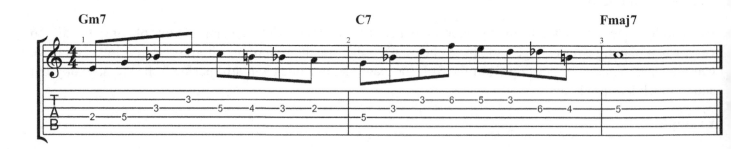

In bar two of this example, you'll recognise the approach of displacing the first note of a phrase by an octave. Here, the first four notes spell a Bbmaj7 arpeggio. Refer back to the arpeggio section in this chapter and you'll recall that Bbmaj7 is the arpeggio built from the b7 chord tone of C7.

Example 3z

This example begins with the exact same idea, but this time played over the Gm7 chord. The second half of this phrase contains the E note again to suggest a Gm6 harmony. In bar two, the first four notes spell a C7 arpeggio, played with octave displacement.

Example 3z1

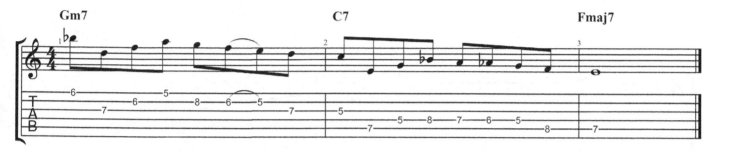

Bar two of this line also features the C7 arpeggio, and the line ends with an enclosure that targets the 7th (E) of the Fmaj7 chord.

Example 3z2

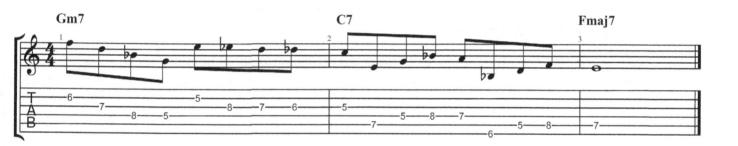

Here's a twist on a classic bebop lick. You'll recognise the sound and shape of the lick, but extra chromatic notes have been added to give add momentum as it descends.

Example 3z3

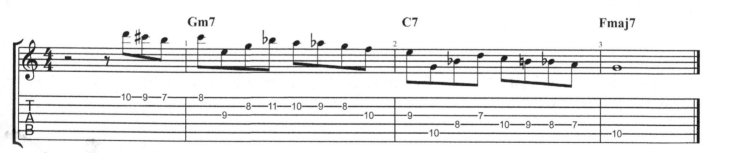

This idea begins in the pick-up bar with an idea you've seen before: a scale tone above, a scale tone below, then a chromatic note below, before we hit the E target note on beat 1 of bar one (which we now know is the 6th of G minor). This is followed by a long chromatic run down. In bar two, a string skip makes the line sound less predictable.

Example 3z4

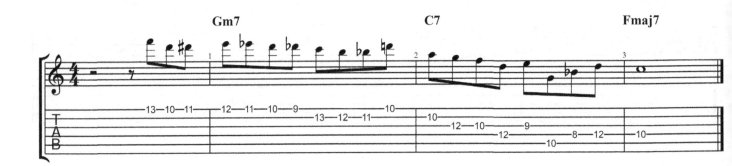

Here's an ascending motif idea for you to try. Beginning on the root of the Gm7 chord in bar one, the lowest note ascends the fifth string chromatically with each four-note phrase.

In bar one, the first phrase is a Gm7 arpeggio. This is followed by a Ddim7 (D F Ab B) arpeggio. In fact, I was thinking of the Dm6 (D F A B) sound of the harmonised dominant bebop scale, but needed to change the A note to Ab to create the ascending low note pattern.

In bar two, the pattern of the first four notes spells an Am7 arpeggio (chord iii in the key of F Major) and the second four spell a Bbmaj7 arpeggio (chord IV). The line ends on a G note, which over an Fmaj7 chord is the 9th.

Example 3z5

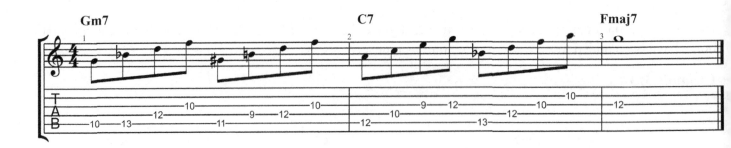

This line uses descending Fmaj7 and Gm7 inversions to form the phrase over C7 in bar two and land on the 7th of Fmaj7 in bar three.

Example 3z6

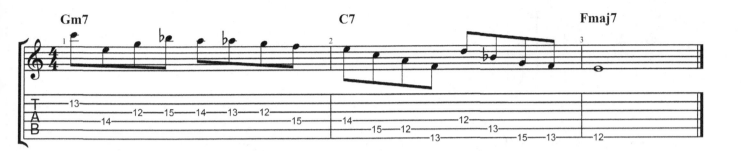

And finally, a descending arpeggio idea. We begin with an Fmaj7 inverted arpeggio at the beginning of bar one, launching from its E note (implying the Gm6 sound again). The next four notes contain a surprise chromatic Eb at the end, which can be interpreted as a G minor b6 arpeggio.

Example 3z7

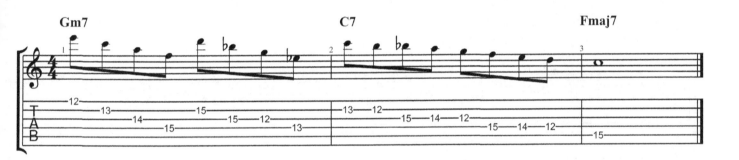

Now it's time for a series of more challenging 1/16th licks, played over the ii V I in F Major. As always, don't worry if, for now, these feel a bit too quick for you. Play through them slowly and study each example carefully, treating it as an etude in its own right. It's more important that you capture the phrasing ideas and begin to absorb them into your jazz vocabulary than it is to play quickly.

It's helpful to frame each idea in terms of a CAGED position around which we can access arpeggio notes, scale tones and chromatic notes.

To get started, the line in bar one of this example is built around the CAGED "A" shape. In bar two, we shift positions down into the "C" form. The diagrams below provide a reminder of the shapes. (The "C" shape is down in 3rd position for this lick).

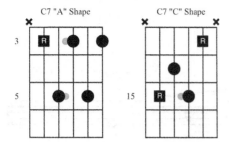

C7 "A" Shape C7 "C" Shape

In bar one, the C Dominant Bebop scale is used almost exclusively, apart from one chromatic passing note near the end of the bar.

In bar two, we return to an idea we've used before: to play the melodic minor scale a half step above the root of the dominant chord, to quickly access the sound of the Altered scale. Here, the notes come from the C# Melodic Minor scale (C# D# E F# G# A# B#).

In bar three, C7, Dm7 and Am7 arpeggios are the building blocks of the line.

Example 3z8

This line opens with a different kind of enclosure. Different musicians have expressed different "rules" for using enclosures, to make a kind of formula, but while this is helpful, the only real rule is that we *target a strong chord tone on a down beat*. If we do that, we can take liberties with the notes surrounding the target.

Here, we play a chord tone above, a chromatic note a half step above, then a chromatic note a half step below the target note of D, which is the 5th of Gm7.

In bar one, the first four notes are an inverted Em7b5 arpeggio (i.e. an arpeggio built from the 3rd of C7). We've seen that this stack of notes can also be seen as an inversion of Gm6, which fits nicely over the G minor chord. Then we descend across the strings with a repeating pattern, aiming for our next target – the Ab note that falls on beat 1 of bar two.

In bar two, we are playing around the C# Melodic Minor scale again to create altered tensions over the C7 chord. Over C7, the G# note that launches the run is the #5. Superimposing C# Melodic Minor over C7 also gives us b9, #9 and #11 tension notes to play with.

In bar three, we're back to the bebop scale with a couple of added passing notes to conclude the line.

Example 3z9

The next example begins with a straight descending C Dominant Bebop run, which is based around the "G" form of CAGED.

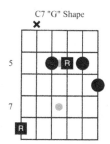

The line in bar two is a mash-up of bebop scale notes and C# Melodic Minor notes. When I played it, I was not thinking so much about note choices as the *shape* of the lick, seeking out the tension notes within easy reach of the "G" shape above.

In bar three, the first four notes spell an Am7 arpeggio (chord iii in F Major), and the line ends on a B note on the first string. Over an Fmaj7, this note is the #11, which gives the line a nice unresolved sound.

Example 3z10

The next line also uses the "G" form and pushes just one fret above it into the higher zone of the neck. In bar one, the opening phrase spells a Gm9 arpeggio, then we descend the bebop scale to target the E note on beat 1 of bar two, the 3rd of C7.

Bar two begins with an inverted Fmaj7 arpeggio, then we sidestep smoothly into C# Melodic Minor for the next cluster of notes, then back into the bebop scale as we cross into bar three. It takes some practice to be able to visualise different scales around each CAGED shape, so it's worth using a free online note mapping tool to investigate where all the notes are located. This makes it easier to practice slipping between the parent scale and the superimposed melodic minor pattern.

Example 3z11

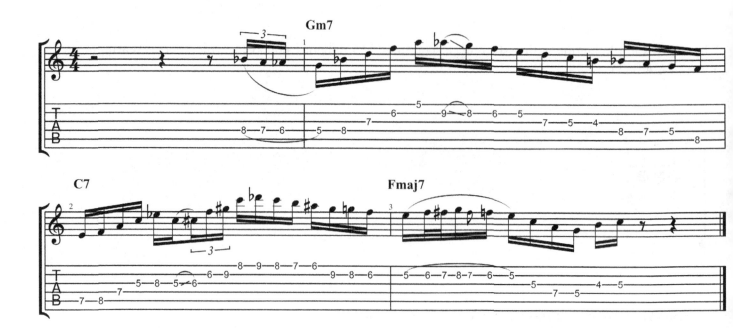

After an enclosure idea in the pick-up bar, this line begins with a C7 arpeggio, followed by a descending run containing some passing notes. In bar two, we play a C# Melodic Minor scale sequence. The last note of the bar resolves to an A note on beat 1 of bar three. This is the first note of an Am7 arpeggio, which is followed by an Fmaj7 arpeggio. After a short chromatic phrase, the lick ends with an enclosure targeting another A note (the 3rd of Fmaj7).

Most of this lick falls into the "E" shape, though there is some crossover with the "G" shape.

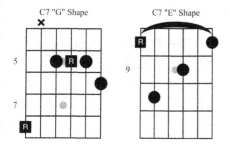

Example 3z12

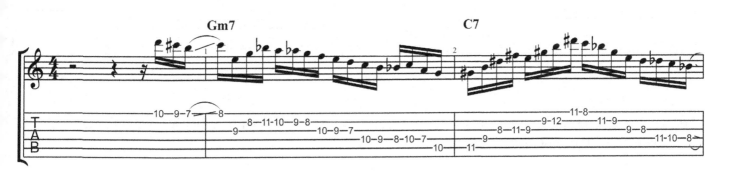

This lick begins with a legato phrase. Downward pick the G note on the second string, 8th fret, then hammer on and roll your fingers upwards from the first to fourth finger. Downward pick the A# note at the 11th fret, then pull off, rolling the fingers back down to return to the G note.

Bar one uses the dominant bebop scale, while bar two has an ascending C# Melodic Minor sequence. Bar three uses the Am7 arpeggio again to start the line. We're using the dominant bebop scale again here, but you'll hear an enclosure idea halfway through the bar, which targets the A chord tone on beat 4.

Example 3z13

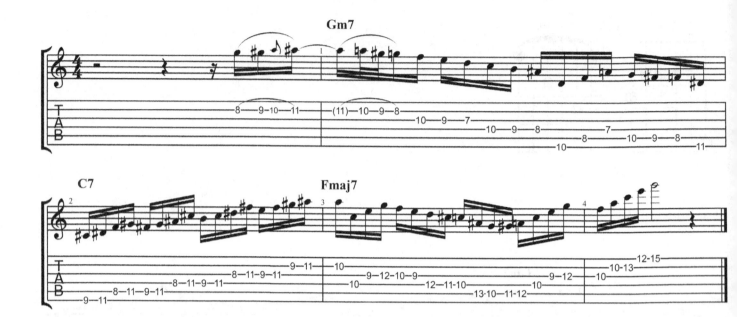

For the next example we move into the higher register of the neck for a line that begins in the CAGED "D" shape and transitions into the "C" shape.

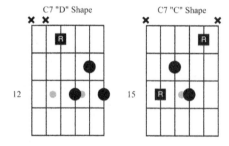

The next lick opens with a longer enclosure pattern.

First, we target the scale tone below the target note by approaching it from a half step below (G# to A), then play two scale tones above (the bebop B note to A), then play the A note again before resolving to the Bb note on beat 1 of bar one. It's a nice six-note phrase, which makes it less predictable than, say, hitting one note on the 4& of the pick-up bar.

Bar one starts with an octave displaced Bbmaj7 arpeggio. Superimposed over a G minor chord it creates a Gm9 sound. After this, another enclosure targets the E note on beat 3, which yields a Gm6 sound. The next target note is the Bb on beat 4 (the 3rd of G Minor), which is approached by a scale run.

In bar two, this is another pattern-based line which uses sidestepped C# Melodic Minor notes to transition from the "D" form into the "C" form to complete the run.

Example 3z14

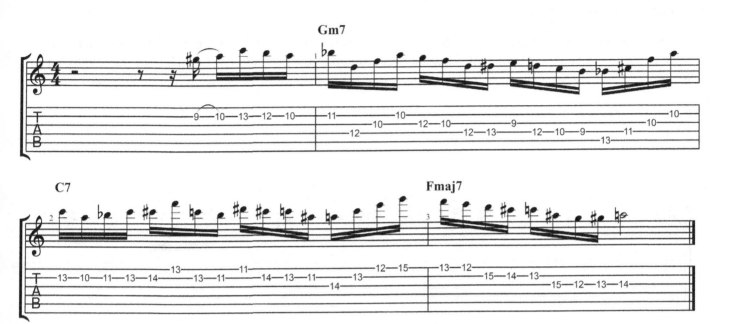

Here is a line that opens with a motif statement with a moving top line. Notes on the G string descend, while the rest remain the same. The first cluster is a G minor triad. By moving the top G note down a half step, we create a GmMaj7 arpeggio. Moving it down one more half step yields a Gm7 arpeggio. We move down another half step for the last phrase of the bar, but this time ascend the arpeggio, which is a Gm6.

Taking a static shape and moving one line (descending or ascending) is a great way of generating melodic ideas. Experiment with this idea and see what you can come up with. You can base it around any chord shape.

Example 3z15

Here's a line that descends with the bebop scale in bar one and ascends in bar two using predominantly C# Melodic Minor scale tones. Positionally, this line is the reverse of the last one, beginning in "C" form and transitioning down into "D" form.

In bar three, the first four notes spell an inversion of Dm6 (remember the harmonised bebop scale arpeggios from earlier in the chapter, which alternate between inversions of C7 and Dm6?). This is followed by an Am7 inversion. Next comes a short scale sequence, and an enclosure to finish lands on the 3rd of Fmaj7.

Example 3z16

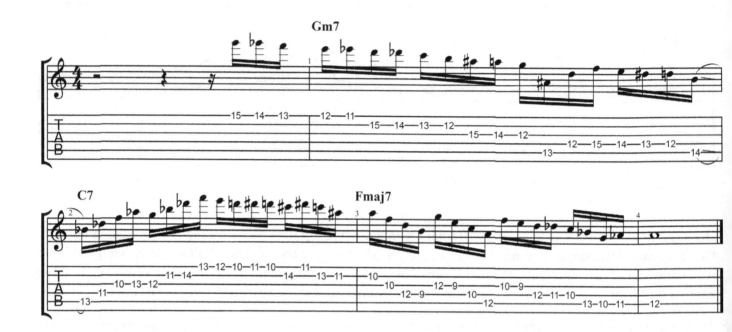

To close out this chapter, here's a line that starts with a C Dominant Bebop descending scale sequence to begin and uses the scale notes to construct an enclosure at the end of the bar that targets the G chord tone (5th of C7) at the start of bar two. Bar two uses the favoured C# Melodic Minor scale to create an inside-outside tension.

In bar three we play a pattern we've used a few times to create melodic ideas: two descending arpeggios followed by a chromatic run down, and an enclosure to finish. Here, the arpeggios are an inverted Am7 and an inverted Bbmaj7.

Example 3z17

We've spent a lot of time exploring the melodic possibilities of the bebop scales in the context of the all-important major and minor ii V I progressions. In the final two chapters, we'll see how to apply some of these melodic ideas to a blues and the changes of a well-known standard.

Chapter Four – Bebop Blues Performance Solo

In the final two chapters, we'll look at two complete performance solos that illustrate how to use bebop scale ideas in the context of a solo.

These solos were improvised, and my aim was to use a variety of ideas and devices found in modern jazz. Alongside bebop scale phrases sit other jazz vocabulary, such as playing arpeggios from different chord tones, emphasising specific chord tone tensions – such as the b9 or b5 – and superimposing pentatonic and blues scales. I hope that this approach allows you to understand how to integrate bebop scale ideas naturally into your playing and to use them when appropriate.

In this chapter, we have a blues in the key of F, based on the chord changes to the well-known Charlie Parker tune, *Billie's Bounce*.

I want to draw your attention to the passages in the solo where bebop scales are used and explain my approach.

First, look at bars 13-16 of the solo, the beginning of the second chorus. Bars 13-14 feature a staple bebop phrase you may have heard played by Charlie Parker, which is built around the F Bebop Major scale (F G A Bb C Db D E). Additional chromatic passing notes are added that target scale tones. The Db bebop note appears in bar 16 and is used to begin the next phrase that crosses the bar line into bar seventeen.

Example 4a

Next, take a look at the idea found in bars 25-28. This is a chordal idea based on the C Minor Bebop scale.

First of all, let's address the issue of why we are playing a C minor bebop scale over an F7 chord. This is a common substitution idea that has been used extensively in the playing of Wes Montgomery and Pat Martino. A key part of Pat's approach was to "minorize" every chord. In other words, he chose to see every chord, whether major, minor, dominant or diminished, as some form of *minor chord type*, so that he could play his favoured minor scale ideas over it.

Both Pat and Wes often played minor ideas a perfect 5th above a dominant 7 chord. In this case, for an F7 chord, they would *think* C minor – a perfect 5th interval away.

So, what is the effect of superimposing C minor over F7?

Cm6 contains the notes C Eb G A.

F7 comprises the notes F A C Eb.

Cm6 shares three notes with F7 (A C Eb) then adds a G note. Over F7, the G note is the 9th.

So, playing a Cm6 arpeggio over F7 gives us the 5th, b7, 3rd and 9th (C Eb A G) of the dominant chord. It's like playing an F9 arpeggio from its 5th, omitting the root note and adding in the 9th, but requires much less thought to achieve the same goal!

Other flavours of C minor chord work too, and have subtly different effects over the F7 chord. A Cm7, which has a Bb note, creates an F11 sound.

A Cm11 chord contains the notes C Eb G Bb D F. Over F7, in order those notes create the following intervals: 5th, 7th, 9th, 11th, 13th and root.

You can see that superimposing a minor chord a 5th above a dominant chord is a quick route to access many colourful extended tones and is an easy substitution to remember.

Now, let's take this idea a step further. If we can use this idea to play melodic lines, can we also use it to play chordal ideas? Absolutely!

Here is a reminder of the C Minor Bebop scale notes:

C – D – Eb – F – G – Ab – A – B

Remember that if we harmonise the bebop minor scale, we get a series of minor 6 chord inversions. Here, we use a Cm6 shape to play a chordal idea over F7. The Cm6 voicing occurs at the end of bar twenty-five and is approached chromatically from below. Another inversion of Cm6 occurs at the end of bar twenty-six.

A good way to practice this idea is to make yourself an F7 chord loop for backing, then play four-note C minor voicings over the top to hear the effect. Try Cm6, Cm7, Cm9 and Cm11 shapes and see what sound most appeals to you.

Example 4b

The last section I want to show you before we move on to the full performance is in bars 32-35 of the solo. I've extracted part of this idea below. The first three bars of Example 4c are the section of the tune that precede the two-bar turnaround.

Here, I play the D Bebop Dominant scale for the Am to D7, ii V movement. Remember that the dominant bebop scale is based on the Mixolydian scale. The notes of D Mixolydian are D E F# G A B C, and the bebop note is added between the b7 and the octave (C#).

Bar thirty-two is a perfect eight-note bebop idea. The first four notes are the D Bebop Dominant scale descending chromatically from the root, then I alter just one note of the scale (lowering the 6th to a b6, B to Bb) for the next four-note phrase. Over D7 this idea has an augmented flavour and creates a sound similar to a D7#5.

Example 4c

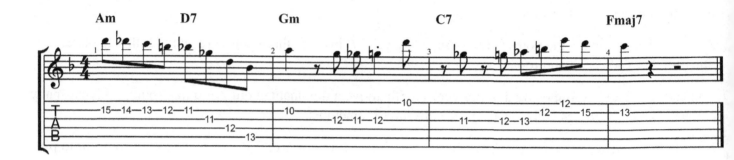

Now have a careful listen to the audio for the full solo and try it yourself.

A good approach here is to break down the solo into two or four-bar sections and learn *complete phrases*, before joining them together. When you're ready, play through the whole solo slowly and begin to train your muscle memory with the required movements.

Also, feel free to just steal any licks that you like and absorb them into your playing right away.

Have fun with it!

Example 4d – Full Solo

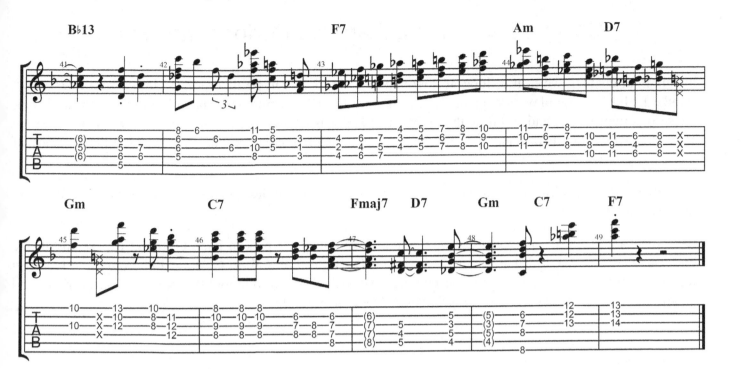

Chapter Five – Jazz Standard Performance Solo

In this final chapter, we turn to look at how bebop scale ideas can be incorporated into a solo over a jazz standard. Here we are playing over the chord changes to the ever-popular standard, *Autumn Leaves*. Again, the solo is improvised, and this time the main idea I had was to play and adapt a series of motifs to build the solo. Using short motifs provides a highly melodic approach to soloing and helps to spell out the harmony of the tune.

As well as the motif ideas there are, of course, passages of bebop scales included, and I'll draw your attention to these bars below.

Example 5a shows the first four bars of the solo (excluding the pickup bar). Over the Cmaj7 chord, the line uses the CAGED "C" scale shape as its basis. The notes come from C Major Bebop, but the lick also features approach notes that target the scale tones. As you've seen throughout this book, we can work around a particular shape and choose any notes that are accessible around it.

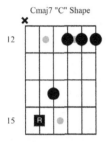

Example 5a

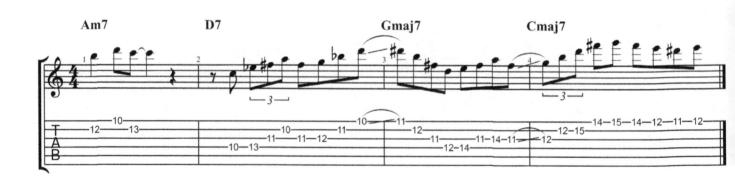

The next example highlights bars 5-12 of the solo. In the first three bars, over the minor ii V i section, all the notes come from the E Bebop Minor scale (E F# G A B C C# D#), which are used to continue the motif idea.

In bar four, anticipating the change to the Am7 – D7 part of the chord sequence, we switch to the D Bebop Dominant scale (D E F# G A B C C#), with a focus on the dominant chord.

Example 5b

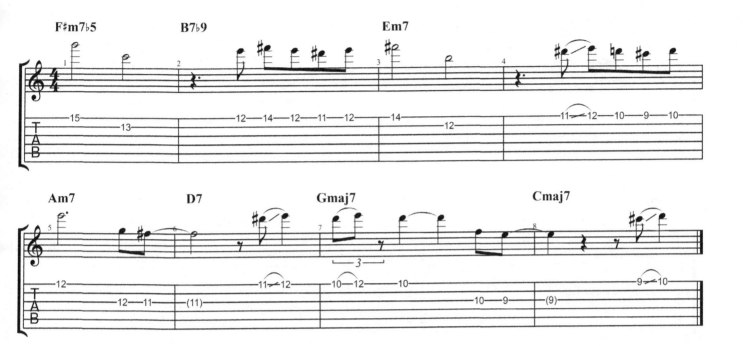

The final example extracts bars 13-20 from the solo. It's another example of the E Bebop Minor scale being used, this time over the extended minor ii V i section of the tune.

Example 5c

Now listen to and begin to work through the full solo. As mentioned, it's a motif study, so there will be lots of useful phrases here that you can adapt into your playing. Break it down into sections to learn, as before.

Example 5d – Full Solo

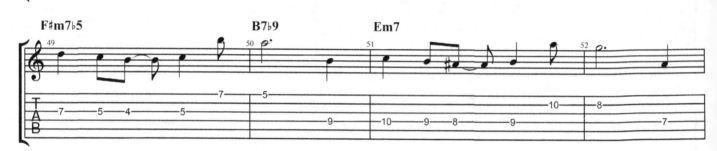

Conclusion

I hope you have enjoyed this in-depth look at bebop scales. They are the basis of so much of the language of the bebop masters, that it's essential to know them inside out if you are serious about mastering this music. Bebop scales are the starting point for creating an unlimited vocabulary of modern jazz licks and phrases.

One of the great myths of guitar playing is that improvisation is a spur-of-the-moment invention. In fact, improvisation can and should be practiced! And the more practice you do, the more the language will naturally come out in your playing. A great starting place to practice your bebop scales is to take a jazz standard you are very familiar with and work on just a few bars. Study the chord changes and work out the CAGED shapes that fit the progression. With this framework in place, you can begin to add combinations of scale tones and bebop scale notes to form melodic phrases around each chord.

Once you are able to play lines around each chord shape individually, the next step is to begin linking them together – to actually play *through* the changes, moving from one shape to the next. When you have practiced a ii V I sequence in one zone of the fretboard, next move it to a completely different zone. Find the new CAGED shapes in that zone and begin again, until you can successfully play through the changes in that area of the neck.

The more you repeat this process, the more fluent you will become at playing anywhere on the fretboard, and the more melodic ideas you will generate – because each zone of the neck has its own sound and shapes that naturally occur.

Keep playing and practicing and I hope to see you at a gig sometime soon.

Ciao,

Eleonora

About the Author

Eleonora Strino grew up in a creative household. Her father and sister were important painters of figurative art, but music was what attracted her. She began playing guitar as a teenager, and from the first time she heard Jim Hall playing with Bill Evans, she knew she wanted to be a jazz guitarist.

She studied at the conservatory in Naples, then at the Conservatorium van Amsterdam with Martijn van Iterson, Jesse van Ruller, and Maarten van der Grinten. Eleonora began her professional career as first guitar in the orchestra of Italian composer Roberto De Simone.

She met Greg Cohen during an audition in Berlin. He was Tom Waits' long-time bass player, and had also played with Ornette Coleman, Lee Konitz and Woody Allen, among others. He took Eleanora under his wing and they started a collaboration that led them to play all over Europe at many important festivals. In 2017, they recorded the album Si, Cy – a tribute to American songwriter Cy Coleman. They continue to tour Europe periodically.

In 2018, Eleonora received an invitation from the renowned Italian pianist Dado Moroni, who has carried on the Oscar Peterson legacy, to be part of one of his bands. They played at leading Italian festivals with American vocalist Adrianne West, who previously worked with Barney Kessel and Joe Pass. In 2020, the Moroni band hosted a week of concerts and masterclasses in Switzerland.

Eleonora is also a composer and arranger. In October 2019, she won a prize for the best composition at the international Johnny Răducanu jazz festival in Romania (named after the Romanian jazz pianist), with her song Senza e Ce Sta. She was invited to play her music with Milan's civic jazz band in the beautiful Strehler Theatre.

In 2021 she was invited to join Emanuele Cisi's new project and in September that year recorded the album Far Away for Warner Music. In addition to the recording, a docufilm will be produced and broadcast on Netflix.

In October 2021 she went on a month-long tour of Germany and Holland, performing twenty-four concerts in thirty days in major theatres and jazz festivals with three other international guitarists (from Russia, Germany and Australia). The tour was arranged by prominent American manager Herschel Freeman, who had called her to be part of the important International Guitars Night tour of North America.

In November 2021 she recorded a new solo project, I Got Strings, which was produced in Berlin by Cam Jazz, and features Joey Baron on drums and Greg Cohen on double bass.

In July 2022 she was invited by internationally renowned guitarist Martin Tayler to play a trio performance, along with world-famous guitarist Ulf Wakenius on The Great Guitars tour – a project that began in 1973 and still continues to this. Over the years it has featured some of the greatest guitar players in jazz history, including Barney Kessel, Kenny Burrell, Herb Ellis, Larry Coryell, Tal Farlow and more.

In November 2022, Eleonora took part in the sixth Tenerife International Guitar Festival, and in the same month began the Women and Music tour – the farewell tour of artist Ornella Vanoni.

In December 2022 she participated in the first Salvador De Bahia International Guitar Festival, where she also held a masterclass at the music conservatory. Eleonora also teaches jazz guitar in Cosenza at the Sanislao Giacomantonio conservatory.

In March 2023, her book Bebop Scales for Jazz Guitar was published by music educator Fundamental Changes, and will be distributed worldwide.

During her career, she has collaborated with musicians including, Wayne Escoffery, Martin Taylor, Ulf Wakenius, Seamus Blake, Joey Baron, Dado Moroni, Adrianne West, Greg Cohen, Danny Grissett, Dario Deidda, Peter Bernstein, Jesse Davis, Aldo Zunino, Enzo Zirilli, Adam Pache, Emanuele Cisi, Rosario.

Eleanora is pursuing many current solo projects. The future is bright for this multi-talented artist.